Martin John Morris

Department of Psychology

University of Melbourne

Minor Thesis Comprising one part of the final assessment

for the Degree of Master of Arts (Clinical Psychology)

Thesis Supervisor: Dr. P. Pattison

February 1987

Burnout in a State Government Construction Authority:

Further Development, Analysis and Predictive Correlates of a

Job Burnout Inventory

Martin Jonn Morris

University of Melbourne

Running Heading:

Burnout in a Government Authority.

Table of Contents

Table of Contents Continued

Table of Contents Continued

Table of Contents Continued

Table of Contents Continued

ABSTRACT

The burnout phenomenon has been extensively studied among human service workers. Although widely acknowledged to be associated with individually and organisationally dysfunctional outcomes burnout lacks substantial theoretical and empirical foundations. Claims have been made that burnout is not confined to the experience of human service workers but is prevalent among those working in corporate sector organisations: employees of large bureaucracies supposedly being particularly susceptible. Very little empirical evidence exists in support of the foregoing assertions. Ford, Murphy and Edwards (1983) developed a perceptual Job Burnout Inventory (J.B.I.) designed to assess the experience of burnout among a wider range of occupations than human service workers. They concluded that human service workers and corporate sector employees process information about stressful job conditions in different ways. Ford et al. (1983) were unable owing to the limited size of their sample to present an analysis of the inventory for any demographic subgroups of human service workers or corporate sector employees. To further establish the efficacy of the J.B.I. and present relevant sociodemographic data, using a 16 item Modified Job Burnout Inventory (M.J.B.I.), including three items to assess expectations of self efficacy at work, data was collected from 440 female and 720 male employees of a large government sector civil engineering organisation as part of their voluntary participation in a broader enquiry into the Status of Equal Employment Opportunity in the organisation.

Subjects were all females in the organisation and a stratified random sample, estimated to be representative, of males. The first two components comprising the factor solution of the M.J.B.I. closely approximated a forced two factor solution reported by Ford et al.(1983) for corporate sector employees.

A significantly smaller proportion of total variance than that reported by Ford et al. (1983) was accounted for by the first two factors of the M.J.B.I. A third factor was revealed describing expectations of self efficacy at work. Results suggest that the M.J.B.I. may be improved by addition of items to measure feelings of personal accomplishment at work.

Tentative support was found for two models of burnout. Each of these models, one causal and the other developmental may be further enhanced by more precise operational definition and measurement of constituent variables.

Subscale scores of the M.J.B.I., sociodemographic variables and work satisfaction measures derived from the Equal Opportunity Survey Questionnaire,and previously reported to be significantly associated with the experience of burnout among human service workers,were included in a multiple regression analysis. Adequacy of the task related communication process between employees and their supervisors was found to be the most powerful predictive correlate of the first two subscales of the M.J.B.I. for both sexes. Components of previously reported significant predictors of burnout among human service workers included in this variable suggested that the experience of burnout among corporate sector employees may be closer to that of human service workers than was conjectured by Ford et al. (1983).

Young employees of both sexes reported significantly lower expectations of self efficacy at work.

The first two subscales of the M.J.B.I. were significantly related to occupational type suggesting that some previously reported significant relationships between burnout and sociodemographic status may have been confounded with occupational status in the samples. Occupations with highest average scores being subjectively judged as those with less formal task structure.

The term "Burnout" was coined by Freudenberger (1974) to
describe conditions of pronounced fatigue, frustration and
psychological strain resulting from the stress of human service work.

Since Freudenberger (1974) and Maslach (1976) defined the
concept as a separate entity burnout has become an increasingly
popularized notion and is now commonly accepted to occur, not only as
an outcome of work related stress and strain among human service
workers, but also in public service and managerial positions where
clients and employees impose constant demands for attention (Farber,
1983). Burnout has come to be associated with a range of individually
and organisationally dysfunctional outcomes including diverse
psychological and physical manifestations. Further than this, Etzion
(1984 p. 615) asserted that burnout has become an important occupational
factor in the "total life and environmental pressures that affect the
individual's well-being".

The central purpose of this study of burnout in an historically
stable male dominated technical bureaucracy was to establish more
clearly the evidence for burnout in such a population. A second
objective of the study was to identify the "high risk" groups for
burnout in the organisation and examine the best predictors of each of
its components.

Characteristics and Historical Development

of the Burnout Construct

Study of the relationship between work and the psychological well being of individuals in industrial societies grew steadily from the early 1960's. Increasing research interest in this relationship coincided with apparent growth in the incidence of work absenteeism owing to psychological maladjustment. Kearns (1973) reported that in the fifteen year period ending in 1973, a period of economic expansion, full employment and relative job security, absence from work owing to physical illness was estimated to have increased in industrial societies by 22%. This is a small increase compared to that of 152% for men and 302% for women attributable to the neuroses and psychosis. The incidence of psychotic disorders is estimated to have remained relatively constant during that period suggesting that the marked increase in work absenteeism was due mainly to the neuroses. It was against this background of increasing incidence and awareness of an apparent deterioration in psychological well being owing to stress at work that burnout had its origins as a separate construct.

Perlmann and Hartmann (1982) conjectured that growing awareness of burnout in the previous few years probably reflected in part the increased importance of human services delivery to government departments and private sector employers.

Descriptive definitions and conceptualizations of burnout have become prolific and the term has found its common acceptance through self-help books such as The Work/Stress Connection : How to Cope with Job Burnout (Veniga and Spradley, 1981) and Burnout:From Tedium to Personal Growth (Pines, Aronson and Kafry, 1981). Farber and Heifetz (1982) predicted that the term Burnout could become a catch phrase of the 1980's, a prediction which despite lack of theoretical and empirical precision in support of burnout, has been shown to have had substance.

The burnout construct is estimated to have received increasing attention in the past 5 years. A N.I.H.M. (1982) database search (American Psychiatric Association Library, Note 1) included references to 78 articles on burnout up to and including 1981. A University of Melbourne literature search prepared in 1985 included reference to 103 articles on the subject in the preceding four years (University of Melbourne, Note 2).

Burnout was originally conceptualized to describe the outcomes of stress particularly associated with human service work. Berkeley Planning Associates (1977) asserted that human service jobs impose demands on workers that are very different from those in other types of work. To a greater extent than in other professions, they argued, human service workers must use themselves as the technology in attempting to meet the needs of clients.

Perlman and Hartman (1982) conceptualized burnout as a multifaceted experience of chronic emotional stress. They expressed the opinion, shared by Meier (1983) that burnout has been primarily, if not entirely, a descriptive term yielding little insight into causation, prevention or cure.

The construct validity of burnout is not yet beyond question. Meier (1984) pointed out that the relationship between burnout and older constructs, such as depression and job satisfaction, while it is substantial, need not reflect either a common aetiology or developmental sequence.

Freudenberger (1974) described depression as a symptom of the burnout process. Weiskopf (1980) cited in Meier (1984) suggested that depression is in fact the final state of burnout. Such relationships have been variously cited, sometimes as a cause and sometimes as an effect; in either case until the discriminant validity of the burnout construct is adequately established the possibility remains that burnout is merely a new name for one or more old phenomena.

Etzion (1984) suggested that burnout is now well documented descriptively but is still in the embryonic stage of empirical study and theoretical clarification.

In a comprehensive review of the burnout literature from 1974 Perlman and Hartmann (1982) cited 44 definitions from 48 sources. Most of the definitions cited by Perlman and Hartman (1982) included reference to emotional exhaustion, cynicism and loss of commitment to work. Other definitions included reference to boredom, depression, dehumanisation, illness, self destructiveness, absenteeism and staff turnover as components of burnout. Only 3 of the 48 studies cited by Perlman and Hartman (1982) referred to burnout among persons other than those in the helping professions and none of these presented data in support of their conclusions. Definitions of burnout by the authors of these studies were not discernibly different from those reported for human service workers.

Pines, Aronson & Kafry (1981) described the burnout syndrome as being characterised by feelings best described as "giving more than is reciprocated". In the vast majority of cases, they assert, the major cause of burnout lies in the work situation. This is brought about they say by the individual having to contend with long periods in which there is at least a lack of positive reinforcement and not infrequently persistent negative reinforcement at work.

Although commonly accepted to occur as an outcome of work related stress, Perlman and Hartman (1982) pointed out unresolved differences of opinion in the burnout literature as to whether burnout is a cause, a process or a consequence of stress.

Writers on the subject are similarly divided, as Perlman and Hartman (1982) have observed, on hypothesized underlying primary dimensions of the burnout syndrome. It is therefore not surprising that Einsiedel and Tully (1981) described the dozens of individual and organisational components of burnout as an unwieldy universe.

Pines et al. (1981) asserted that for burnout to occur at all the individual must at some time early in his or her career have been "on fire". Such a metaphor implies a zealous commitment to the intrinsic value of the work. Among human service workers this may be a relatively common phenomenon. For employees in the majority of occupations it is almost certainly the exception rather than the rule. This potentially distinctive feature of human service work may well account for the special research interest generated by the burnout phenomenon in this group. Pines et al. (1981) argued that burnout is not exclusively the experience of human service workers. In conditions of frustration and role overload employees in bureaucratics, and some commercial enterprises, are vulnerable to burnout. They reported that the incidence of burnout is most likely to be high in large organisations in which the autonomy of the individual is eroded by formalised hierarchial decision processed. In such organisations self reported job satisfaction is least likely to be high and the onset of burnout most rapid. A prerequisite for burnout, one which is claimed to differentiate this condition from the job alienation of some blue collar workers, is initial idealism, excitement, and high expectations concerning work outcomes. For this reason burnout most often occurs to people who initially cared least about their pay cheque.

The Relationship Between Occupational Stress, Strain and Burnout

Occupational stress, strain and burnout have been reported in their respective literatures to share many of the same causes, symptoms, dysfunctional outcomes and suggested remedies. (Sharit and Salvendy, 1982; Perlman and Hartman, 1982). Since these concepts overlap, and there is lack of agreement on operational definitions for any of them, it would seem premature at the present time to treat burnout as an independent research domain.

Sharit and Salvendy (1982) pointed out that the number of factors qualifying as potential sources of occupational stress is seemingly limitless. They concluded that stress among white collar workers is essentially multifactorial requiring focus on more than one stressor at a time. The tendency among authors to think about the problems of stress from a single causative perspective is, they argued, more a reflection of biases in the scientific orientation of these authors than adherence to the boundary conditions of any particular theory.

Sharit and Salvendy (1982) suggested that the definition of stress proposed by McGrath (1970) has had the widest acceptance. McGrath (1970) defined stress as a perceived substantial imbalance between demand and response capability under conditions where failure to meet the demand has consequences which are perceived to be important by the person experiencing stress. Stress, by this widely accepted definition, describes a state of the individual. Operational definition of stress according to this widely accepted descriptive definition presents many of the same problems common to other definitions of the phenomenon. Principal among these is the requirement for reliable measurement of variables hypothesized to be essential components of stress. Properties of the environment which are assumed to be causally implicated in the experience of stress are usually referred to as stressors and reliable measurement of these is essential since all later inferences are derived from this measurement.

Sharit and Salvendy (1982) argued that the degree of fit between person and environment determines the degree of either coping or maladaptive behaviour and subsequent stress related symptoms. They concluded their review of occupational stress with the assertion that demands of the work situation and the range of decision making discretion available to the worker facing these demands accounts for the level of strain. If any one variable were to be singled out as the predominant underlying source of occupational stress it would in their view be uncertainty. If goals are felt to be unclear, and feedback on performance inadequate, it is to be expected in their view that the experience of subjective stress will be more intense. They observed that uncertainty will probably become a more prevalent source of occupational stress as people are increasingly working with systems about which they know very little.

The term strain has been used by other authors, e.g. Kahn (1973), to describe the affective reaction of the individual to stressors. Operational definitions of strain face many, and perhaps more, of the same problems as those for stress. Burnout will be conceptualized as a component of strain for the purposes of this study since it has so far been measured principally by self reports of negative feeling states associated with the work situation. Reasons for the emergence into popularization of the semantically vivid terms "Burnout" and "Tedium" (Pines, Arouson and Kafry, 1981) are obscure. They do however reflect the difficulty in providing an adequate operational definition of the diverse and unpleasant emotional experience each of them was coined to describe independently of the situations in which they occur.

Operational definitions of the burnout pheno....non have rarely been attempted and it was not expected that anything approaching a complete operational definition of burnout could be developed from results of the present study. It was anticipated however that data from the present sample of public sector corporate employees would suggest rational criteria for experimental study aimed at operational definition of burnout in organisational settings.

The field of occupational stress research is an older and scientifically more rigorous progenitor of burnout research. Ganster, Mayes, Sime and Tharp (1982) observed that little had been achieved other than general agreement that stress at work is a critical determinant of employee health and well being and has important implications for the effectiveness of organisations and the society in which they operate. They concluded that even well formulated and executed stress management programs are of dubious value in coping with chronic organisational stress and reiterated the pressing need for rigorous evaluation of stress management techniques expressed by Newman and Beehr (1979). Newman and Beehr claimed in their review of stress management techniques that the scientific study of the causes of stress was meager, and that virtually all such techniques depended on subjective assessments of effectiveness, few having been evaluated with any rigour.

Physical manifestations of burnout among human service professionals reported in the literature have included many of those previously associated with work stress. Symptoms reportedly associated with burnout have included chronic fatigue, nausea , accident proneness, sexual problems, ulcers, headaches, backaches and increased frequency of minor infections (Edelwich and Brodsky 1980). Maslach and Jackson (1981) reported having identified a number of potentially serious consequences associated with burnout in the course of their research among human service workers. These included low morale, absenteeism, job turnover, sleep disorders, licit drug abuse and family conflict.

The extent to which a causal relationship exists between some or all of these dysfunctional correlates and burnout is largely unknown. The cost of each, both in terms of individual suffering and organisational inefficiency, is undoubtedly considerable. Where statistics are available they almost certainly represent only a small fraction of the hidden cost to society.

Of those most frequently affected by work related stress and strain recently in Victoria, only 3 of the 10 occupations with the highest incidence of statistically recorded stress, among males and females, were human service workers. Included among other occupational groups with the most frequently reported claims for Workcare compensation arising from work related stress were government and non government clerical workers of both sexes, stenographers, typists and office machine operators, male agricultural managers and office cleaners of both sexes (Victorian Workcare Report 1986).

The occupational group most frequently referred to in the work related stress literature prior to 1975 was management. Gowler & Legge (1975) concluded that much of the occupational stress among those with responsibility for the work of others is the product of the following four principal factors.

1. Uncertainty of outcome,

2. The importance of that outcome for the individual,

3. The individuals perception of their ability to influence
   that outcome,

4. Lack of clear criteria for success.

Each of these factors is closely parallel to frequently hypothesized causes of burnout.

Pines et al. (1981, p.208) reported a summary of occupational differences in the overall level of burnout. In general the groups described as management reported among the lowest average burnout scores compared to teachers, nurses and other human service workers. Berkeley Planning Associates (1977) reported that the supervisors of human service workers were significantly less likely to be burned out than the people reporting to them. These results suggest the possibility that burnout at least in human service organisations, is either comprised of components other than those to which management are vulnerable, or that managers are better equipped for some reason to cope with the determinants of burnout.

In common with many employees in public and private sector organisations, arguably to a greater extent than most, subjects in the present study have in recent years worked in conditions of increasing change. With change comes uncertainty and Galbraith (1973) has argued that increased uncertainty creates more exceptions to established rules and procedures in the organisation. The result he asserts is a greater demand on decision makers at all levels in the organisation.

The relationship between such increased demands and burnout is almost certainly a dynamic one in which some, perhaps most of all those who must make decisions in conditions of change within the framework of unchanged policy, are more prone to experience burnout than others. Such a position would be consistent with the view that burnout, an apparently psychologically complex phenomenon judging by the descriptive definitions of it, constitutes part of the change process itself.

Folkman (1982) reported that sixty percent of stressful events occurring in paid work involve interactions with a colleague. This finding supports the view expressed by Newman and Beehr (1979) that stress phenomena have the dynamic open system characteristics of all human action in social settings. In this regard they maintained the symptoms of stress will only be resolved by improving the fit between the person and environment. Burnout can thus be viewed, in common with other forms of strain, as a symptom of poor fit between person and environment in conditions of change and uncertainty.

At least one author, Gertz (1979) cited in Perlmann and Hartmann (1982), has considered the possibility of whole organisations becoming burned out. It seems feasible that burnout phenomena, whatever their aetiology, possess system characteristics reflecting processes of the broader socio-technical system in which they occur.

It may not be fanciful to conjecture, given the increasingly pervasive nature attributed to the phenomenon by Pines, Aronson and Kafry (1981) and Maslach and Jackson (1981), particularly in large bureaucratic organisations, that burnout constitutes only a small part of a broader sociotechnical system dysfunction associated with increasing structural change. Such propositions must of course remain nothing more than conjecture, at least until the burnout phenomenon, if indeed it is a separately identifiable phenomenon, can be specified with a great deal more clarity than hitherto.

The Unresolved Debate on the Causes of Burnout

Pines, Aronson and Kafry (1981 p.3) described burnout as "an insidious general erosion of the spirit", brought about in the vast majority of cases by too many environmental pressures, conflicts and demands combined with too few rewards, acknowledgements and successes. Such general erosion of the spirit is most likely to occur they said among those who were, at least in the early years of their careers, among the most enthusiastic. They further asserted that the syndrome is not confined to those who work in the helping professions. Perceived lack of personal autonomy among employees in large bureaucracies, together with frustration arising from poorly planned change and frequent amendments to operating procedures, are claimed by Pines et al. (1981) to be common antecedents of burnout. Such lack of perceived autonomy and consequent frustration is frequently aggravated by ineffectual communication processes in the organisation according to these authors.

Maslach (1982) suggested that although personality variables play some role in the development of burnout they are much outweighed by the importance of situational sources of job related interpersonal stress. The phenomenon is so wide spread, and those affected so numerous and heterogeneous in personality, that it makes no sense in her view to identify particular personality types as special cases of burnout. For Maslach (1982, p.9) "the stress of the job is the cause".

Perlman and Hartman (1982) categorised the hypothesized causes of burnout reported in the literature they reviewed into individual and organisational variables. Twenty-nine articles cited both "individual" and "organisational" causes of burnout. Fourteen authors cited only organisational causes of burnout while three attributed burnout exclusively to the individual.

Many researchers have equated stressors with the cause of burnout but few have attempted to test this proposition. The few empiricial studies that exist invariably use a narrow range of haphazardly chosen predictors. The notion of stressors in the work place causing burnout is merely self fulfilling and fails to explain either individual differences in burnout or the, as yet unexplored, occupational variation suggested by Pines et al. (1981) and Maslach and Jackson (1981).

Although it has become a pervasively tacit assumption in the literature that the variously reported manifestations of burnout owe their existence to the effects of organisational stressors, Meier (1983) described the current status of burnout theory as a void, and proposed a theoretical model in which prolonged low expectations for reinforcement on the job can lead to burnout. The tentative model proposed by Meier (1983) is based on the interaction of individual and organisational variables. It was thus an attempt to resolve what he considered a fruitless debate regarding the causality and maintenance of the burnout experience.

The Measurement of Burnout

Pines, Aronson and Kafry (1981) stated that burnout and the condition named by them "Tedium" are both states characterized by physical, emotional and mental exhaustion. Tedium is considered by these authors to be identical to burnout with respect to definition and symptomatology. The Tedium measure developed by Pines et al. (1981) consists of twenty nine variables judged to reliably describe the burnout syndrome. Cumulatively these items provide a single burnout score.

Maslach and Jackson (1981) developed the Maslach Burnout Inventory (M.B.I.) to measure burnout among human service professionals. The M.B.I. consists of three principle subscales of burnout. The first of these, Emotional Exhaustion, describes feelings of being emotionally overextended and exhausted by work. The second subscale, Personal Accomplishment, describes feelings of competence and successful achievement : lower scores on this subscale correspond to higher experienced burnout. The third subscale, Depersonalisation, describes unfeeling and impersonal responses to those for whom human service care is provided. The M.B.I. thus produces scores on non additive components of burnout.

Maslach and Jackson (1981) reported that the first four factor subscales of the M.B.I. accounted for more than three quarters of total variance. They did not however report the percentage of variance explained by any of the individual factors in a heterogenous group of human service workers.

Belcastro, Gold and Hays (1983) used the Maslach Burnout Inventory to study burnout among teachers and reported an almost identical item factor structure to that reported by Maslach and Jackson (1981). Emotional Exhaustion, the principal factor identified by Belcastro et al. (1983) accounted for less than 25% of total variance.

Belcastro, Gold and Hays (1983) noted that the rate at which the Maslach Burnout Inventory (Maslach and Jackson, 1981) had been utilized in occupational stress research among human service workers increased markedly in the two years following its publication. The psychometric soundness of the instrument, they asserted, had been demonstrated to be satisfactory. In particular, they claimed that the MBI is not simply another index of job satisfaction, neither is it subject to distortion by social desirability response sets. In a study of 826 teachers, Belcastro et al. (1983) reported burnout factor scales closely consistent with those reported by Maslach and Jackson (1981) for a heterogeneous sample of human service professionals.

Golembiewski, Munzenrider and Carter (1983) contended that burnout among human service workers and those employed in commercial enterprises can be reliably measured using the M.B.I.

Stout and Williams (1983) compared the two measures of burnout in most common use at that time. These were the Tedium Measure (Pines, Aronson and Kafry 1981) and the M.B.I. (Maslach and Jackson 1981). They concluded that the Tedium Measure may not be as sensitive in assessing the relationship between burnout and other variables with which it has been identified including role conflict, work ambiguity, qualitative and quantitative work overload among others.

Ford, Murphy and Edwards (1983) observed that nowhere in the scientific literature at that time had the burnout phenomenon among managers, engineers, scientists, technicians, clerical and administrative workers been addressed. In order to understand the nature of the burnout syndrome among corporate employees and compare this with that experienced by human service workers Ford et al. (1983) developed a 15 item Job Burnout Inventory (J.B.I.). This was designed to measure the following aspects of burnout hypothesized to be common to both human service workers and the broader range of corporate sector employees.

a) The experience of emotional exhaustion arising from
excessive demands on energy, strength and resources,

b) Demoralized frustrated feelings and reduced efficiency.

It was the intention of Ford et al. (1983) to contribute to the development of an inventory capable of measuring the experience of burnout with reliability among a wide range of occupations. They claimed that neither episodic stress nor chronic job stress were related to burnout in a sample of 150 clerical, supervisory, technical and management personnel employed in a variety of private sector corporations. On the basis of their results they felt able to confidently reject the possibility that the job burnout inventory they designed and used in their study was synonymous with other measures of stress and strain.

Ford, Murphy & Edwards (1983) suggested that human service professionals process information about stressful job conditions differently to some extent from employees in corporate sector settings. They found differences in the factor structure derived from a corporate sector sample compared to that produced from the responses of human service professionals to their Job Burnout Inventory. These differences, they conjectured, stemmed from the nature of the attributions each occupational group makes about the bases of stressful conditions in the work environment.

Ford et al. (1983) omitted reporting data on percentage of variance explained by the first factor in their original four factor solution of burnout among corporate sector employees. In the Ford et al. (1983) study, Emotional Exhaustion and Defeat emerged as the principal factor for corporate sector subjects only in a forced two factor solution.

Maslach and Jackson (1981) established that feelings of lowered personal accomplishment were a component of burnout among human service workers. Ford et al. (1983) made no attempt in their Job Burnout Inventory to examine the relationship between the subjective experience of burnout and feelings of lowered self efficacy and personal accomplishment. Since Ford et al. (1983) anticipated developing a burnout inventory suitable for use among a wide range of corporate and human service employees the omission of items designed to measure lowered personal accomplishment seems an unwarranted exclusion. Perhaps more easily understood is their reasoning for omitting items relating to the third scale of burnout identified by Maslach and Jackson (1981). Depersonalisation, the third factor subscale after Personal Accomplishment in the Maslach Burnout Inventory (Maslach and Jackson 1981) is arguably unlikely to contribute substantially to burnout among corporate sector employees. The five items in the M.B.I. Depersonalisation subscale described unfeeling and impersonal responses to those receiving human service care. For this reason the Depersonalisation subscale is largely irrelevant to the assessment of burnout among almost all corporate sector employees. It is felt however that any inventory designed to measure the experience of burnout in a wide range of occupational groups, including human service workers, would be incomplete without at least two or three of the more important Depersonalisaion items. In respect of the absence of items relating to Depersonalisation and Lowered Personal Accomplishment the Job Burnout Inventory developed by Ford et al. (1983) must be considered deficient.

The research of Berkeley Planning Associates (1977), Perlman and Hartman (1982) amd Maslach and Jackson (1981) provide support for conceptualizing burnout as a multi-dimensional construct which, when measured, cannot simply be aggregated into a gross burnout "Score".

The results reported by Ford et al. (1983) provide further confirmation that burnout is not an homogeneous phenomenon but that one or more of its components may be shared across populations. The implications of this apparent lack of homogeneity in the burnout construct present substantial difficulties, not only in theory development but also, in the absence of a viable theoretical model, establishing with reliability which groups are at risk for burnout and under what conditions the pheonomenon may be preventable or the effects mitigated.

In the light of the different factor structures of burnout reported by Ford et al. (1983) for human service workers and private sector corporate employees it seems likely that a useful operational definition of burnout in corporate sector organisational settings will be developed only following further refinement of instruments for measuring burnout. The present study was designed to establish the usefulness of the J.B.I. to measure burnout among different demographic and occupational subgroups in a large public sector organisation.

Burnout in Organisations

Burnout has not been widely studied in bureaucracies or private sector organisations. This is suprising as it has been associated with a range of individually and organisationally dysfunctional outcomes among human service workers. A wide variety of prescriptions for remediation of burnout have been advocated none of which have been reliably validated. These have included an apparently determinist and fatalistic acceptance that the best employees, even in flexible organisations, are most likely to burn out periodically and at these times "can be given something different to do" (Pines, Aronson and Kafry, 1981, p. 114). The same authors have suggested that employees experiencing burnout adopt active, confronting coping strategies. An active confronting coping strategy is described by Pines et al. (1981, p. 157) as one in which the employee (a) adopts a positive attitude. (b) confronts the source of stress. (c) changes the source of stress. The advocacy by Pines et al. (1981) of such remedial strategies to cope with what they describe as a "general erosion of the spirit", p. 3, precipitated by undefined chronic negative reinforcement at work suggests an element of "blaming the victim".

Golembiewski, Munzenrider and Carter (1983) argued that even job enrichment strategies will often generate stimulus overload among those already experiencing the emotional exhaustion hypothesized by these authors to be the final stage in burnout.

Meier (1983) recognised that the prescription of appropriate interventions to alleviate the effects of burnout was tantamount to prescribing cures for an unknown disease. He alluded to the growing suspicion surrounding burnout: that we do not really know what burnout is or how it is related to other more clearly defined concepts like job satisfaction and depression.

The construct validity of burnout may not yet as Meier (1984) concluded be beyond question; what is less in doubt is its criterion validity. In support of this assertion Etzion (1984) reported five studies in which subjects self reported burnout was significantly correlated with co-worker evaluations. Etzion (1984) concluded that since differences exist in individual coping strategies, before generalisations are drawn and prescriptions for organisational intervention formulated, special attention should be paid to occupational and sex differences in burnout.

Gertz (1979) conjectured that whole organisations may reach the stage of burnout. Little is known in support of this conjecture concerning the aetiology, incidence or developmental stages of burnout in organisations. If the constellation of conditions under which burnout is most likely to occur can be established, the developmental stages of the phenomenon, hypothesized to exist by Golembiewsky et al. (1983) may be more reliably predicted and its dysfunctional effects minimised.

Ford, Murphy & Edwards (1983) pointed out that very little attention in the growing body of stress literature had been focussed on job burnout among corporate employees in either the private or public sectors. They expressed the view that a better understanding of the processes of burnout in these populations would have important consequences for the field of work related stress.

Relationship Between Burnout and Work in Organisations

Job Satisfaction

Role conflict and ambiguity in work settings have been repeatedly found to be negatively correlated with psychological and physical well being (Van Sell, Brief and Schuler, 1981).

Maslach and Jackson (1981) reported a moderate but statistically significant negative relationship between burnout and job satisfaction. Since less than 6 percent of variance was accounted for by any of the relevant correlations they concluded that while burnout is not independent of job satisfaction it is certainly not a synonym for it. They also reported each scale of the M.B.I. to be independent of social desirability response set among human service workers.

Ford et al. (1983) found significant relationships between subscales of burnout, as measured on their Job Burnout Inventory, and several work outcomes measured using well known and reliable instruments. The extent to which these relationships were statistically significant differed between the human service workers and corporate sector employees. Among corporate sector employees, significant negative relationships were reported by Ford et al. (1983) between the first subscale of the J.B.I. Emotional Exhaustion and Defeat and the following work outcomes : satisfaction with work, supervision, pay, promotion opportunity, informational support, and degree of role ambiguity. A significant positive correlation was reported between this subscale and role conflict.

A significant negative correlation was reported between scores on the second J.B.I. subscale of burnout, Resource Inadequacy, and satisfaction with supervision. A significant positive correlation was found between this subscale and role conflict. Correlations between Resource Inadequacy and satisfaction with work, pay, promotion opportunity, informational and structural support failed to reach a statistically significant level. The correlation with role ambiguity also narrowly failed to achieve statistical significance among the corporate sector subjects in the results reported by Ford et al. (1983).

In general, the negative correlations reported by Ford et. al. (1983) were stronger between Emotional Exhaustion and Defeat and job satisfaction than those reported by Maslach and Jackson (1981). Each of them, they averaged - .35, could still be described as moderate. Present methods of measuring burnout all rely on self report of negative feeling states at work and thus inevitably share common variance with constructs other than job satisfaction such as depression and anxiety. Until more precise methods of measuring the components of what has been demonstrated to be a multifaceted phenomenon can be developed it seems likely that the problem of discriminant validity will remain an impediment to progress.

Communication

Muchinsky (1977) examined relationships between organisational communication, organisational climate and job satisfaction in a large public utility. He concluded that the individual who has a positive feeling about communication within the organisation also has positive feelings regarding the organisation's psychological environment and management in general.

Porter and Roberts (1976), in a review of organisational communication processes, concluded that the employees' immediate supervisor is the most important source of communication affecting task outcomes. Synder and Morris (1984) emphasized the view that communication processes underlie and are critical to effective organisational functioning. They drew attention to the paucity of research studies attempting to explain the relationship between communication variables and overall performance at both the individual and organisation level.

In a study of public service employees Synder and Morris (1984) assessed two aspects of supervisory communication: overall effectiveness of the supervisor as a communicator and adequacy of performance feedback provided by the supervisor. They concluded that the supervisor's effectiveness as a communicator contributes more to overall organisation effectiveness than adequacy of the performance feedback provided to the individual by supervision. Their results suggested performance feedback is of greater importance for individual feelings of self efficacy.

In a study of the sources of job stress among 800 young graduate engineers, Keenan and Newton (1985) found that by far the largest source of stress related to respondents' feelings that either their time, or their efforts, or both had been wasted or used ineffectually by their organisation. Keenan and Newton provided examples of the type of responses made by engineers. The following two accounts were judged typical of responses from this group. "After working on a design for two weeks the spec. was changed. Then after working on the new spec. for 1 day the spec. was changed back to the original." Another said: "I spent several days helping the purchasing department solve a parts shortage. They failed to let me know that they had found a suitable supplier. It appeared that they were unconcerned at wasting days of my time. I received no apology". p.154.

Keenan and Newton (1985) evaluated by factor analysis the relative strength of feelings about the sources of stress and found "Frustration and Anger" to be the principal component. This was followed by a second smaller factor labelled "Anxiety/Uncertainty" and a third labelled "Underload".

The results reported by Keenan and Newton (1985) suggest that a frequent response to stress arising from inadequate communication is frustration and anger. This result is consistent with that reported by Drabek and Haas (1969) cited in Newman and Beehr (1979) who found that the primary stressor in conditions of uncertainty arose from overloading the communications network. Keenan and Newton (1985) pointed out that frustration and anger reactions to chronic stress have rarely been investigated; much research having been limited to anxiety type phenomena.

The relationship between organisational communication variables and burnout is by no means clearly defined. It would be reasonable to expect, on the basis of the literature reviewed by Van Sell et al. (1981), that role ambiguity and the stress and strain associated with it could be ameliorated by efforts to improve communication processes in the organisation. Contrary to the expectation that role clarification would follow increased frequency of staff meetings, Jackson (1983) reported a slight increase in role ambiguity among hospital nursing staff when the frequency of such meetings was increased. Jackson concluded that her results suggest that the amount of job related communications that occur is determined by role conflict and ambiguity.

Berkeley Planning Associates (1977) reported the perceived quality of organisational communication to be a significant predictor of burnout among human service workers. Since there does not appear to have been comparable research in any corporate sector organisation

the present study was designed to explore the relationship between
burnout and perceptions of the adequacy of communication in a large
public sector corporate organisation.

Feedback on Performance

Maslach and Jackson (1981) found a significant relationship
between all three subscales of burnout reported in their study and
feedback received from supervisors on job performance as measured by
the Job Diagnostic Survey (Hackman and Oldham 1975) . Maslach and
Jackson (1981) predicted from the earlier results of Maslach (1976) that
human service workers scoring high on burnout would not know how
effectively they were performing their jobs. Low scores on the Job
Diagnostic Survey Subscale of "knowledge of results" were
significantly correlated with each of the subscales of burnout.
Maslach and Jackson (1981) concluded that the work outcomes of low feedback
and lack of knowledge of results justified their prediction that high
scorers on burnout would not know how effectively they were performing
their jobs. The implications of this state of affairs, both for the
individual in the organisation, and the organisation itself are self
evidently serious. If individuals in private or public corporate
environments such as the RCA, are burned out and unaware of their own
level of effectiveness it seems probable, on the basis of the
existing burnout literature, that they will be resistant to any
attempts made to change those features of the organisation which, if
they did not bring about burnout in the first place, at least support
the phenomenon through ineffectual communication. Resistance to
change may result, as Golembiewski et al. (1983) have suggested, from

stimulus overload among those experiencing emotional exhaustion.

Contrary to their expectations, Ford, Murphy and Edwards (1983) reported that the structuring of activities by supervisors, as measured by the Leader Initiating Structure scale of the Leader Behaviour Description Questionnaire (Stogdill, 1963), was negatively correlated with burnout among human service workers. Among corporate employees Role Conflict was also significantly correlated only with the Emotional Exhaustion and Defeat subscale of burnout. The correlation between Role Ambiguity and the Resource Inadequacy scale of burnout failed to reach statistical significance. Ford et al.(1983) concluded that, while human service workers appear to process information about stressful work conditions somewhat differently than corporate sector employees, supervisors efforts to limit role ambiguity have significant strain reducing effects for both groups.

Snyder and Morris (1984) speculated from the general pattern of their results that self perceived adequacy of performance may be influenced by the process of performance feedback from supervisors. Taking their speculation a step further : the adequacy of performance feedback may influence individual expectations of self efficacy at work. If such a relationship exists it follows that the significant relationships reported by Ford et al. (1983) between the first subscale of the J.B.I., Emotional Exhaustion and Defeat, and the measures used to assess perceptions of Informational Support at Work and Role Ambiguity may be considered supportive of the model of burnout proposed by Meier (1983). In this model low expectations for self efficacy at work are postulated to lead to overgeneralization errors and thus burnout.

In the event that satisfaction with performance feedback received and self efficacy expectations at work are found to be independent it suggests that the persistent negative outcome expectations postulated to influence the development of burnout in Meier's model are more influential in determining burnout than those for self efficacy. Such speculation is not intended as any test of the model but in view of the theoretical complexity of its components, and Meier's own suggestion that initial exploration of the role of self efficacy expectations might proceed with a self report measure, the relationship between satisfaction with performance feedback and self efficacy expectations was examined only speculatively.

Opportunity for Personal Growth and Development

Maslach (1976) and Maslach and Jackson (1981) reported a significant negative relationship among human service workers between burnout and dissatisfaction with opportunity for personal growth and development on the job. The level of satisfaction with opportunity for personal growth and development on the job was measured in their studies using the "Growth Satisfaction" scale included in the Job Diagnostic Survey (Hackman and Oldham 1975).

Occupational Differences In Burnout

The literature on burnout has consistently alluded to the possibility of significant occupational differences in the phenomenon. As yet the relationship between burnout and occupational status in corporate sector employees has remained unexplored.

The observation that males included in a structured interview program reported higher levels of uncomfortable stress at work in the RCA (Morris, Note 3) is consistent with the result obtained by Billings and Moos (1982). Billings and Moos (1982) developed a work environment scale including measures of perceived stressful aspects of the job milieu. They found that work stressors had a greater impact on men in a representative community group. This result is at variance with the results reported by Maslach and Jackson (1981) and Etzion (1984). Females in each of these studies were significantly more burned out than males. Maslach and Jackson (1981) cautioned that the significant sex differences in burnout reported in their study may have been confounded with occupational type. It was an objective of the present study to clarify the relationship between the subscales of burnout, to the extent this is measured by the J.B.I., and occupational type.

Pines, Aronson and Kafry (1981) reported a summary of occupational differences in the overall level of self reported burnout among human service workers as measured by total scores on the Tedium Measure (Pines, Aronson and Kafry, 1981). Such differences have so far remained largely a speculative explanation for other significant demographic differences: e.g. the sex differences reported by Maslach and Jackson (1981). It was expected that, if the incidence of self reported burnout was found to differ significantly between occupational groups, more specific hypotheses could be formulated concerning the aetiology of the phenomenon.

Correlates of Burnout in the R.C.A.

Research on the predictors of burnout has been limited among human service workers and evidently non existent in any corporate sector group.

Berkeley Planning Associates (1977) reported a multiple regression analysis which revealed that only perceived quality of leadership, organisation communication, caseload size and supervision responsibility contributed a significant portion of the variance in burnout among human service workers. Guided by the results of Berkeley Planning Associates (1977), Maslach and Jackson (1981) and Ford, Murphy and Edwards (1983) it was expected that factor analysis of Equal Employment Opportunity Survey Data (Morris, Note 3) relevant to work outcomes previously reported to be associated with burnout would identify several sufficiently well defined quasi independent variables to be useful in a regression analysis. (Details of quasi independent variables used in the regression analysis appear in the following Method section). It was conjectured that if the burnout construct, as measured by the Modified Job Burnout Inventory (M.J.B.I.), a modification of the Job Burnout Inventory developed by Ford et al. (1983), is comparable among the present sample of public sector corporate employees to that reported among the corporate sector employees in the sample studied by Ford et al. (1983), predictive correlates of the subscales of the M.J.B.I. would share common features with those reported by Berkeley Planning Associates (1977) for human service workers. It was expected that identification of predictive correlates of burnout in the R.C.A. would assist in the development of a strategy for further research into the causes and management of burnout in this and similar organisations.

Any study of burnout and its correlates depending on survey questionnaire data alone will inevitably have to deal with at least three possible explanations of significant correlations. The first possibility is that the significantly correlated variable contributes to causation of burnout: Second, that the significant relationship is an effect, and finally, that the correlation reflects neither cause nor effect of burnout but some other variable present in the sample, itself correlated with burnout. An example is the case of the significant relationship reported by Maslach (1976) and Maslach and Jackson (1981) between Growth Satisfaction and burnout. In this case and perhaps others, all of these explanations is possible. On the one hand it seems unlikely that persons who are satisfied with opportunity for growth and development will be high scorers on any burnout inventory. On the other hand the presence of dissatisfaction with this and other somewhat molar work outcome variables says very little of use in directing more specific future research into the causes and effects of burnout.

It was anticipated that further predictive research on burnout in organisations, based on more rigorous methods of inquiry than self report measures alone, could be facilitated by refinement of some of the predictive variables previously included as independent variables in regression models. Each of the identified predictors of burnout in research with human service workers is in itself a multifaceted phenomenon. Models of the developmental sequence of burnout in organisational settings can undoubtedly be made more specific if the components of them can be described operationally.

Models of Burnout

Using their own measures of stress, strain and coping Osipow & Spokane (1983) proposed a model in which occupational stress, strain and coping are related. Given equal amounts of stress they postulated, strain varies as a function of coping. In a demographically and occupationally heterogeneous sample, Osipow, Doty and Spokane (1985) found no significant sex differences in work related stress or strain. Among older subjects the effects of stress were significantly lower than among younger subjects. This result is consistent with that reported by Maslach and Jackson (1981) who found a lower incidence of burnout among older human service workers. Osipow & Spokane (1983) pointed out that, as in the present study, a) there were occupational membership differences in the sexes, b) women were more highly represented in the younger groups and men in the older groups. Consistent with the model proposed by Osipow and Spokane (1983) results of a multiple regression analysis reported by Osipow et al.

(1985) suggested that strain varies as a function of coping resources.

The onset and developmental stages of burnout have been the subject of mainly speculative model building.

Meier (1983) proposed a model of burnout based on the interaction of individual and organisational influences in the development of burnout. Burnout in Meier's model depends on environmental influences as well as individual outcome and efficacy expectations. The model of burnout developed by Meier was based on the self efficacy theory proposed by Bandura (1977). The model emphasized the cognitive and behavioural aspects of burnout in addition to the affective sequelae. Burnout in this model arises from repeated experiences in which the individual has low expectations of positive reinforcement from work and high expectations for negative reinforcement. Additionally the model suggests that low expectations both for control of existing reinforcers and personal competence have been learned by repeated experience in the work situation.

Expectations of a lack in personal competence on the job thus may lead to overgeneralisation errors and subsequent burnout. While the model is conceptually elegant Meier admitted that interaction of the variables concerned is not well understood. Meier suggested that at least the general predictions of the model might be usefully tested through a self report instrument to measure expectations of self efficacy for correlation with other measures of burnout.

The onset of burnout has been described by Pines, Aronson and Kafry (1981) to be most rapid in large bureaucratic organisations with hierarchially formalized decision making processes. Stout and Williams (1983) conjectured that elevated scores on the emotional exhaustion component of burnout could be expected before depressed personal accomplishment. Others, including Golembiewski, Munzenrider and Carter (1983) have concluded that emotional exhaustion occurs at a later stage in the development of burnout.

Golembiewski et al. (1983) developed a tentative stage model of burnout based upon robust covariation of the component subscales of burnout identified by Maslach and Jackson (1981) with a panel of variables considered to be important aspects of organisational life. Emotional exhaustion constitutes the final stage of burnout according to this stage model. Emotional exhaustion is preceeded by diminished personal accomplishment in their model.

Golembiewski et al. (1983) factor analysed 21 variables used in the construction of their stage model. These variables related to aspects of supervision, conditions of employment and job satisfaction. Included in the 21 items were those comprising the Job Diagnostic Survey (Hackman and Oldham, 1975) they found the following five factors with eigenvalues greater than 1.0.

    I   Supportive supervision that promotes growth,

II Work that is attractive, involving and rewarding,

III Work that is satisfying/meaningful to individuals

and socially integrative,

IV Compensation

V   Work with a high activity level.

They recommended future research to further explore the relationship between these work outcome measures and burnout.

Taking account of the propositions included in the models of burnout proposed by Golembiewski et al. (1983) and Meier (1983) it would seem reasonable to expect that employees reporting high levels of emotional exhaustion will also continue to show evidence of the following earlier developmental stages of burnout. First, the diminished personal accomplishment proposed by Pines et al. (1981) to precede emotional exhaustion and second, the lowered expectations of self efficacy predicted by Meier (1983).

Supportive evidence for the general predictions of the model of burnout proposed by Meier (1983) was reported by Stevens and O'Neil (1983) in a study of human service workers. Stevens and O'Neil (1983) examined the relationship between expectations for client progress and burnout among human service workers. High expectations were significantly related to low burnout. Burnout was reported as being preventable when workers shifted from reliance on expectations of client progress to improved self efficacy in the work.

In this study it was practicable only to estimate expectations of self efficacy at work. This was achieved by inclusion of three additional items in a Modified Job Burnout Inventory.

The Relationship Between Burnout and Demographic Variables

The recent literature on burnout among human service workers has reported a number of significant relationships between scores on the subscales of burnout, particularly emotional exhaustion, and sociodemographic subgroups. Authors of these studies have invariably added well justified notes of caution on the interpretation of such data since the significance of the relationships may easily have depended on the effects of comfounding variables in the samples studied. The equivocal nature of the significant relationships reported so far in the literature, while they do not lend a great deal of support to either side in the debate concerning individual versus organisational causation of burnout, suggest that certain groups may be more at risk for burnout.

Ford et al. (1983) were unable to report analysis of the J.B.I. for any demographic subgroupings owing to the limited sample size of both human service professionals and corporate sector employees in their study. Since they found a different factor structure of burnout for each of these groups, concluding from this that corporate sector employees make different attributions concerning the source of stressful job conditions, it seems possible that such differences will be reflected in the relationships between burnout and the sociodemographic subgroupings of corporate sector employees previously reported among human service workers. The present sample of public sector corporate employees, although drawn from a single organisation, was considered to be of sufficient size and heterogeneity to make these relationships worthy of report. In particular because it has been suggested by Maslach and Jackson (1981) that occupational differences may have accounted for some of the previously reported variation in burnout scores.

The range of occupational status in the present sample, while not directly comparable to that reported by Maslach and Jackson (1981), was diverse and broadly representative of a wide range of the corporate sector population in public service for both sexes. It was expected that if significant differences in burnout were observed between occupations in the present inquiry this information would have value in at least two respects. First, potentially fruitful avenues of further investigation concerning the aetiology of burnout would be suggested by the characteristics of those occupations with the highest and lowest burnout scores. Second, the organisation has limited resources to apply to an occupational health care program. The identification of groups at particular risk for work related strain will assist those responsible for the allocation of limited resources to make more effective decisions.

Gender

Osipow, Doty and Spokane (1985) noted that the literature on stress, strain and coping at work has invariably reported women experiencing more stress and strain in the workplace than men.

Contrary to their expectations they found no sex differences in work strain as measured by their personal strain questionnaire among 310 subjects from a wide range of occupations.

To the present author's knowledge, where significant sex differences in burnout have been noted in the literature, females have consistently reported higher levels of emotional exhaustion than males. In a wide ranging sample of over one thousand human service workers with approximately equal numbers of each sex, Maslach and Jackson (1981) reported significantly higher scores among females than males on Emotional Exhaustion, the first subscale of burnout in the M.B.I. Etzion (1984) using a 21 item burnout inventory designed to measure emotional exhaustion reported a similar result to that previously reported by Maslach and Jackson (1981) and concluded that evidence is growing that women, the fastest growing sector of the workforce in industrial societies, experience occupational stress in different ways to men.

Etzion (1984) argued that not only do women have a different experience of stress to men but the coping strategies they adopt differ as a result of gender differences in socialization processes. In a study of Israeli managers and human service professionals of both sexes Etzion (1984) found that women experienced more burnout and stress in life than men but found no such sex differences for stress in work. Burnout among males and females in Etzion's study was moderated by different variables. Burnout among males was moderated by supportive relationships in their work environment while women relied predominantly on sources outside the work place: family and friends.

Being principally a civil engineering organisation, requiring many technical employees to be geographically mobile within the state, the R.C.A. has historically been predominately a male culture. This has been changing at an accelerating pace in recent years as more female graduates from a variety of disciplines take up roles previously the exclusive domain of males. Following a statement of E.E.O. objectives the results of an opinion survey of employees on matters relating to equal employment opportunity (Morris, Note 3), showed that not only were women significantly less satisfied than men with a wide range of factors affecting their employment but men were significantly more likely than women to express the view that it would be more difficult for a woman to obtain promotion. Because job satisfaction has been consistently reported to be negatively correlated with burnout (Meier, 1984), it was expected that females in the present organisation would report significantly higher levels of burnout.

Age

Osipow, Doty and Spokane (1985) observed that little is known about life span occupational stress and strain. They questioned whether there are substantial differences across the life span in these variables as has been shown to be the case with job satisfaction (Van Mannen & Katz, 1976).

An inconsistency in previously reported burnout research of particular relevance for the present study is the relationship between burnout and age. Several studies, including those reported by Berkeley Planning Associates (1977) and Maslach and Jackson (1981) have found burnout to be significantly related to age; younger human service workers of both sexes being more likely to experience burnout than older workers. Gann (1979) also found age rather than length of time in the job significantly related to burnout.

Metz (1979) in a study of teachers found males between 30 - 49 self reported significantly more burnout while females in the same age group reported significantly greater self renewal.

Cardinell (1981) suggested that certain career development stages are ripe for burnout because commitment to work ideals may be significantly larger than the sense of satisfaction from work at these times. A mid career "crisis" has been suggested to occur after the "establishment life stage", reflecting a career disruption when adequacy of life style is re-evaluated (Golumbiewski, 1978).

Since little is known about the incidence of work related stress and strain across the life span, and results in the burnout literature are equivocal, it was not possible to entertain anything but the most general expectation that the weakest relationship could be expected among older employees of both sexes.

Marital Status

Maslach and Jackson (1981) reported a statistically significant relationship between the emotional exhaustion component of burnout and marital status. Single and divorced persons scored higher than those who were married. In presenting their results on this relationship Maslach and Jackson combined the sexes; thus it was not possible to make any comparison between them. Such a comparison, in the light of other reported sex differences in burnout, would have been potentially worthwhile.

Etzion (1984) found that although women experienced significantly more burnout, and more stress in life than men, no such sex differences were apparent for stress in work. Pines, Aronson and Kafry (1981) argued that role conflict is a major source of stress and the main antecedent of burnout among women combining careers with homemaking. The result reported by Etzion (1984) suggests the possibility that the higher level of burnout among women has its origin in the additional role strain imposed on working mothers. This possibility is conjectural since the marital status of females in Etzion's study was not specified. To further explore the relationship between burnout and marital status in the present study results are presented separately for each sex.

Education

Maslach and Jackson (1981) reported a significant relationship between Emotional Exhaustion and level of education. Higher levels of education have been associated with increased emotional exhaustion.

Maslach and Jackson did not report data for each sex separately. In view of the significantly higher level of emotional exhaustion among women in their study it was conjectured that, if a significant relationship emerged between burnout and education in the present sample, the effect would be stronger among females.

Salary

No reference was found in the literature to any relationship between burnout and level of income. The significant relationship between age and Emotional Exhaustion reported by Maslach and Jackson (1981) suggested the speculative possibility that those earning higher salaries, because they are older, would score lower on such a subscale if one emerged as a component of the M.J.B.I.

Research Questions

Notwithstanding existence for over a decade the burnout construct is neither theoretically defined nor empirically broadly researched. Fundamental questions also remain only partially satisfied concerning the construct validity of burnout. Models of the phenomenon have been only tentatively constructed and none of these can be considered to have predictive power.

For these reasons the formulation of empirically testable research hypotheses was considered premature. Until recently only minimal research on the burnout phenomenon in organisational settings, other than in human service agencies, has been reported in the literature. That which has appeared tentatively suggests some dissimilarities in the experience of burnout among corporate sector employees. Results of research to date among corporate sector employees suggested a number of research questions salient to the apparent differences in burnout experience between this group and human service workers.

Dominant among these is the question of measurement of the experience supposed to constitute burnout among corporate sector employees. The J.B.I. developed by Ford et al. (1983) was claimed by those authors to be a reliable instrument. It was a principal objective of the present study to further examine this assertion and present an analysis of the results derived from a M.J.B.I. for several sociodemographic subgroups. Each of these has been previously reported in the literature to be significantly related to the experience of burnout.

Numerous correlates of burnout have been reported in the literature. Among human service workers several groups of these have been reported to have predictive significance. The present study attempted to sufficiently refine some of those predictive correlates known to be of relevance to the work experience of employees in a large public sector organisation. Each of these, together with sociodemographic variables, was used as an independent variable in a multiple regression analysis with the following aims:

(a) To establish and examine the characteristics of the most powerful predictors of each of the subscales of a M.J.B.I. in the organisation. (b) To compare the predictive correlates of any

subscale of the M.J.B.I., which could justifiably be considered a
measure of burnout, with those reported for human service workers.
(c) The formulation of a more precise operational definition of
the burnout construct in a large corporate sector organisation. This
is required for the further development of phenomenological and causal
models of burnout in organisations.

Levels of support for the general predictions of two models of
burnout, one causal and one phenomenological, was examined within the
design limitations of the present study.

Unexplained occupational differences in burnout have been shown
to exist among human service workers. The present sample was
comprised of a wide range of corporate sector occupational status.
The relationship between the subscales of the M.J.B.I. and
occupational status was examined. The suggestion, also unexplained,
that whole organisations or parts of them may be differentially
affected by burnout was also examined by comparing scores on each of
the subscales of the M.J.B.I. at geographically separate work
locations. It was anticipated that tentative explanations of any
differences among either of these subgroups would be possible using
predictive correlates derived from a multiple regression analysis.

Participants in the present study were drawn from 18 different
work locations in the state of Victoria. Of these, 8 are located in
the Melbourne metropolitan district, and 10 in widely dispersed
country towns. Locations vary not only geographically but also to the

extent each is involved in the construction of new roads and bridges as distinct from maintenance of the existing road network. It was not possible on the basis of the existing literature on burnout to formulate specific research expectations concerning differential incidence of burnout. Rather, it was conjectured that burnout would be most in evidence in those locations characterised by higher levels of change.

Method

Study Design, Sample and Setting

The Road Construction Authority of Victoria (RCA), the organisation from which the sample for this study was drawn, has the following notable characteristics. The mission of the organisation, the planning, design and construction of roads and bridges in Victoria has been a stable one. For historical reasons the organisation has become established as a male dominated civil engineering culture. Employees, particularly those with an engineering background and thus a well developed professional and managerial career path, have been able to anticipate long term security of employment together with the possibility of advancement according to ambition and ability. During the working life of most employees the government of Victoria has remained a conservative one and little externally initiated change has influenced internal management decision making processes. Technical, political and socioeconomic development in the past decade have created a more turbulent and uncertain environment for many in the organisation.

The study comprised one part of a broader enquiry into the current status of Equal Employment Opportunity in the RCA. The RCA employs approximately 5000 personnel throughout the State less then 10% of whom are female. An E.E.O. survey was designed to provide the management of the organisation with reliable data upon which an affirmative action plan could be developed aimed at ensuring achievement of the organisation's stated objectives on

E.E.O. The E.E.O. Survey was comprised of 63 questions (213 variables) and was designed to capture a wide range of sociodemographic data as well as information concerning disability, career development aspirations, human resource management practices, training needs, potential for discrimination, conditions of employment, sexual harassment and the experience of stress at work. (The E.E.O. Survey Questionnaire together with accompanying instructions appears in Appendix A.)

Each question was structured in a different format to minimize response set. An untitled 16 item Modified Job Burnout Inventory (M.J.B.I.) was included as the final section of the survey.

At the conclusion of the E.E.O. questionnaire each participant had responded to a wide range of matters relating to their employment with the RCA. It was expected that by including the M.J.B.I. as the final section of the questionnaire each participant would be more likely to respond with an overall view of his or her feelings at work rather than either calling to mind critical incidents or denying negative feelings altogether.

Subjects and Procedure

All 440 female employees of the RCA were included in the survey sample. A stratified random sample of 720 male employees was drawn from personnel records of the RCA existing at the end of October 1985.

Males were selected randomly using a modification of SPSSX (SPSS Inc. 1983)   sampling procedure to include employees from each of the 19 departments in the RCA across all 18 geographic locations throughout the State of Victoria. The sample of males was sufficiently large to achieve approximate representative status of all males in the organisation. Males were classified according to the 9 principal occupational categories. Females were classified according to their membership of the 8 major female employment categories.

The total Survey Sample was thus 1160. Participation in the E.E.O. Survey was voluntary. Females were aware that each would receive a questionnaire and males were informed of the random sampling procedure in a RCA newsletter. Each recipient was encouraged to participate in an accompanying letter from the Chairman of the RCA.

Assistance with English language interpretation was offered to any person requiring this. The anonymity of each participant was assured and summarised feedback on results promised to every employee via the employee newsletter.

Survey questionnaires were dispatched on 3rd December, 1985 to each selected employee using the internal mailing system. Instructions for questionnaire completion and return were included with the survey questionnaire together with a pre-printed envelope for this purpose. Participants were reminded to return completed questionnaires as quickly as possible in an announcement which appeared in the RCA Weekly Personnel Notices on 15th December, 1985.

Fifty-two questionnaires were returned undelivered. The principal reason was that the addressee had terminated employment since the personnel records file used in sample selection had been created. Females who had joined the organisation later than this date and who requested a questionnaire were included in the sample (8). Two respondents, both male, returned uncompleted questionnaire forms together with signed notes to the effect that they disagreed with the objectives of the survey.

Seven hundred and thirty-three completed questionnaires were returned. 468 males participated (65%) and 265 females returned completed questionnaires (60%). The lower response rate for females was contrary to expectations since it is generally recognised in the community that E.E.O. efforts by Government at State and Commonwealth levels are aimed at greater participation in the workforce by females. It was apparent that older married females with longer than average length of service were the least likely to participate in this survey. A precise demographic description of the 170 females who chose not to participate in the survey was not possible without a detailed analysis of personnel records information, a task outside the scope of this study.

Demographic Characteristics of the Sample

The median group for age, in which 18% of male respondents were included, was 35 - 39. The median group for age, in which 24% of females were included, was 25 - 29.

Eighty-nine percent of males and 87% of females described their ethnic group as Australian. Ninety-seven percent of males and 95% of females reported English as their first language. Seventy-three percent of males and 47% of females were married. Males in this sample were thus older and more likely to be married than females. They also had significantly greater average length of service with the organisation; 11.6 years on average compared to 6.1 for females. Males and females in the sample reported a mean of 6.5 years and 5.5 years respectively of relevant work experience prior to joining the RCA.

The median salary group for males was $23,500 - $26,500 per annum. For females it was $17,500 - $20,500 per annum. Sixty-seven percent of males in the survey sample received annual income exceeding $20,500, the national average, compared to 29% of females.

Males had received more years of formal education than females. Sixty-five percent had at least HSC level compared with 50% of females.

Fifty-five percent of males were salaried employees and 45% were wage earners. Seventy-three percent of females were salaried and 27% wage earners. Wages employees of both sexes had a lower response rate than salaried employees. Since 34% of wages males responded, and 19% of wages females, it can be further concluded that wages females were less interested in the survey than wages males.

Males in the sample, as in the whole organisation, were employed in a wider range of occupational categories compared with females. Male and female respondents in this study were classified in the occupational groups listed in Table 1 for data analysis.

Table 1
Percentage of Total Respondents in Each of the
Occupational Groups Used for Data Analysis.

	(% of completed questionnaires)	
	Males	Females
Engineers	22%	3%
Road Building Personnel	19%	–
Drafting Officers	13%	13%
Administrative and Clerical Officers	13%	32%
Scientists and Technicians	10%	9%
Survey Officers	7%	–
Drivers/Storemen/Maintenance Personnel/Others (8 categories)	6%	–
Management and Supervision	5%	–
Non Engineering Professionals	5%	4.5%
Typists/Word Processor Operators	–	26%
Other Minority Occupational Groups (Catering Assistants, Filing Clerks, Stores Assistants) (8 categories)	–	7%
Secretaries	–	5.5%

Forty three percent of females in the sample were employed in the Head Office of the R.C.A. compared to 31% of males. Thirty-two percent of females worked in country districts compared to 46% of males.

Variables and Measures

Each of the variables in the study is identified and its measurement explained below.

Individual Demographic Variables

The variables employed were age, gender, marital status, education level, wage or salaried officer and salary level. Each respondent was asked for these six pieces of data on the E.E.O. Questionnaire.

The Equal Employment Opportunity Questionnaire: Questionnaire Development

Items in the E.E.O. questionnaire were developed from data collected in the course of 78 structured interviews. Forty-eight males and 30 females from a stratified random sample of employees participated in the structured interview program.

The structured interview format was compiled following unstructured interviews with 64 employees.

Participants in the structured interview program were each interviewed by one of ten employees of the RCA (eight females and two males). Interviewers were selected by a joint consultative committee on E.E.O comprised of representatives of both sexes from Staff Associations, a Study Group for Women in the RCA and Management. Interviewers received two four hour training sessions in the use of the structured interview format. Each interview lasted approximately 2.5 hours.

At the conclusion of the structured interview program all interviewers participated in a half day review at which each was able to present the author with additional relevant material.

Participants in the structured interview program were asked to rate the degree of uncomfortable stress experienced at work on a 0 - 100 point scale from "none" to an "extremely high degree". The item relating to uncomfortable stress at work was included in the structured interview format as a result of the frequency with which employees consulted the RCA welfare psychologist concerning problems which they ascribed to stress at work. Males reported higher levels of uncomfortable stress at work than females. Interviewees were asked to expand on their own experience of the sources of uncomfortable stress at work. It was clear from the responses to this item in the structured interview format that uncomfortable stress at work was a source of concern for many employees of the RCA.

The structured interview plan appears in Appendix A.

Structured interview data was analysed and the results presented to the consultative committee on E.E.O. The committee as research clients used these results to guide the item selection and development of the E.E.O. survey questionnaire while the present author acted in the role of research consultant to the committee. The 63 items in the E.E.O. questionnaire covered the following domains. (1) Demographic status. (2) Disability. (3) Employment conditions and the management process in the R.C.A.. (4) Work history, training and career development. (5) Equal employment opportunity issues particularly those affecting women and minority groups.

Qualitative data from structured interviews, in addition to the specific items relating to uncomfortable stress, indicated that many employees regularly experienced feelings at work associated with burnout. A Modified Job Burnout Inventory (M.J.B.I.) was included in the survey questionnaire. The inventory was similar to that developed by Ford, Murphy and Edwards (1983) who designed a Job Burnout Inventory (J.B.I.) capable of measuring burnout among corporate sector employees.

The Modified Job Burnout Inventory

Eleven of the sixteen items included in the Modified Job Burnout Inventory were the same as those comprising the inventory constructed by Ford, Murphy and Edwards (1983). Four items from the Ford et al. (1983) scale were omitted as they were unacceptable to the senior management group of the RCA who considered them to have an unnecessarily negative connotation.

These items from the Ford et al.(1983) inventory were replaced as follows:

Item 3. I feel "emotionally" drained on my job.

Item 4. I feel "Defeated" like I'm up against a brick wall.

Item 10. I am tired of trying.

The items above were replaced by a single item in the Modified Inventory. It appears as item eleven; "I feel uncomfortable stress at work."

Item 8. Efforts to make progress at my job are fruitless

This item was replaced by item 9 in the Modified Inventory; "I feel frustrated by my job".

Results of the structured interview program indicated that many employees had concerns about coping with work pressure, lack of confidence and uncertainty at work. In order to explore the relationship between these self-efficacy concerns and burnout three further items were included in the Modified Inventory as follows:

Item 1. I cope well with the pressure of my work (reverse scored).

Item 3.   I cope well with uncertainty at work (reverse scored).

Item 5.   I feel confident about the quality of my work (reversed scored).

Items used in the Modified Job Burnout Inventory are presented in Table 2. The M.J.B.I. was introduced as follows:

"The following statements relate to some of the ways in which people experience stress at work. Consider the way in which each statement applies to the way you feel at work. Place a number between 1 and 6 in the box to the right of each statement according to the following scale":

1	=	Never True
2	=	Very Rarely True
3	=	Sometimes True
4	=	Often True
5	=	Very Frequently True
6	=	Always True

Table 2:

Modified Job Burnout Inventory Scale Items

_____

1. I cope well with the pressure of my work (reverse scored)

2. No matter what I do, things at work don't seem to get better

3. I cope well with uncertainty at work (reverse scored)

4. I feel used up at the end of the work day

5. I feel confident about the quality of my work (reverse scored)

6. I feel I give more than I get in return

7. I feel a sense of isolation from the rest of my peers, co-workers etc.

8. I generally have sufficient time or resources to do my job (reverse scored)

9. I feel frustrated by my job

10. I experience conflicting demands in my job

11. I feel uncomfortable stress at work

12. I have difficulty attending to family or personal needs

13. I feel unable to express and share dissatisfaction about my job

14. My work load is impossible to catch up

15. My job is such that I can effect little change in the work situation.

16. Temporarily removing myself from the job environment seems to resolve my feelings

Relationship Between Subscales of the M.J.B.I. and Selected Work Measures

Ford, Murphy and Edwards (1983) reported correlations for corporate sector employees between the subscales of burnout on the Job Burnout Inventory and selected work measures. The instruments used by Ford et al. (1983) had been previously validated and each was considered to have very acceptable levels of reliability. The measures included satisfaction with work, supervision, pay, promotion prospects, role ambiguity, informational and task structuring support at work. They found significant negative correlations between the first subscale of burnout on the Job Burnout Inventory (J.B.I.), Emotional Exhaustion and Defeat and each of the above work measures. They reported only one significant negative correlation between the second subscale of burnout on the J.B.I., Resource Inadequacy, and the same measures: that with satisfaction with supervision. Analogous items from the E.E.O. survey questionnaire appear in Table 3. Correlations between these items have been reported separately in order to compare the present results with those of Ford et al. 1983).

Table 3

Work Measures Selected for Comparison with the Results
of Ford, Murphy and Edwards (1983)

E.E.O. Survey Question No.	Item Content
46	Satisfaction with Type of Work
46	Satisfaction with Amount of Work Expected by your Supervisor.
46	Satisfaction with your Working Relationship with your Supervisor.
46	Satisfaction with Quality of Supervision.
46	Satisfaction with your Supervisor's Recommendations on Promotion.
46	Satisfaction with Pay.
46	Satisfaction with Future Prospects.
48	Satisfaction with Goal Clarity.
51	Satisfaction with Feedback on Performance.

Relationship between Disability and the Subscales of The M.J.B.I.

The E.E.O. Survey included a seven part question on disability (Q16). Participants were asked to rate any disability suffered as either severe, moderate or mild.

Other Measures Relating to Present Research Questions

Fifty items from the E.E.O. questionnaire were selected as useful measures concerning present research questions. These items were chosen on the basis of their relevance to previously published research on the relationship between Burnout and the following work domains:

a)   Perceived Quality of Leadership and Supervision

b)   Overall Job Satisfaction

c)   Goal Clarity and Feedback on Work Performance

d)   Effectiveness of Communication in the Organisation.

e)   Opportunity for Personal Growth and Development on the Job.

Twenty-nine of these items were chosen for their relevance to the first four work domains and twenty-one because each reflected a potential component of perceived opportunity for personal growth and career development.

The twenty-nine items selected for their relevance to Leadership and Supervision, Job Satisfaction, Goal Clarity and Feedback on Performance and Communication in the organisation, in order of their appearance in the E.E.O. survey questionnaire were as follows:

Survey Question Number	Item Code	Item Content
25	SELECT 7	Overall adequacy of procedures related to selection for promotion
38	FEEL 1	Overall level of satisfaction with present job
39	FEEL 2	Overall level of satisfaction with amount of responsibility in present job
40	CAREER 1	Extent of availability of career guidance in the organisation
41	CAREER 2	Satisfaction with career guidance received
46	PHYSICAL	Adequacy of physical working conditions
46	PATSAT	Adequacy of paternity leave conditions
46	MATSAT	Adequacy of maternity leave conditions
46	SUPER 1	Adequacy of information provided about the Superannuation Scheme before you decided to join
46	SUPER 2	The degree to which you fully understand the provisions of the Superannuation Scheme
46	PAY	Satisfaction with your current level of pay
46	HOURS 1	Satisfaction with hours worked
46	HOURS 2	Satisfaction with flexibility of hours worked
46	TYPEWK1	Satisfaction with the type of work you do
46	TYPEWK2	Extent to which you find your work interesting and absorbing
46	TYPEWK3	Satisfaction with the amount of work expected of you by your Supervisor

Survey Question Number	Item Code	Item Content
46	TALK 1	Satisfaction with the effectivenss of communication about work related issues between staff and management in your area of work
46	TALK 2	Satisfaction with the effectiveness of communication between co-workers about work related issues in your area
46	SETPRIOR	Satisfaction with your ability to set your own task priorities in your present job
46	SUPERV1	Satisfaction with the working relationship you have with your Supervisor
46	SUPERV2	Satisfaction with the quality of supervision provided by your Supervisor
46	SUPERV3	Satisfaction with your Supervisor's ability to make fair and reasonable recommendations on your promotability based on your work performance
48	CLTYGOAL	Adequacy of work related goal clarity
49	WKSITN	Adequacy of Supervisor's awareness of your current work situation
50	FEEDBK1	Adequacy of your Supervisor's efforts to give constructive feedback about your work
51	FEEDBK2	Satisfaction with the feedback and recognition you receive from your Supervisor about your work
53	ISOLATE	Extent to which you feel "cut off" from others in the organisation
56	GRIEVE 10	Expected adequacy of Supervisor's response in the event of a work related grievance
56	GRIEVE 17	Overall level of satisfaction with grievance procedures in the organisation.

The twenty one items from the E.E.O. Questionnaire selected for their relevance as useful measures concerning present research questions on the relationship between burnout and opportunities for Personal Growth and Development on the Job, in order of their appearance in the E.E.O. Survey, were as follows :

Survey Question Number	Item Code	Item Content
28	SUPRPRO1	Extent of Supervisor's encouragement to apply for promotion
29	SUPRPRO2	Satisfaction with encouragement received from Supervisor to apply for promotion
30	TRNGKNOW	Extent of knowledge of training programs offered by the organisation
31	TRNGNEED	Extent to which training needs have been considered by Supervisor
33	STRNG1	Adequacy of induction training on joining the organisation
33	STRNG2	Adequacy of the "on the job" training received
33	STRNG3	The opportunity to develop skill by attendance of training courses

Survey Question Number	Item Code	Item Content
33	STRNG4	Satisfaction with Supervisor's effort to ensure adequate training for the job
33	STRNG5	Satisfaction with prospects of receiving training to make progress in the organisation
33	STRNG6	Satisfaction with the quality of training courses attended in the organisation
33	STRNG7	Satisfaction with information received concerning training available in the organisation
33	STRNG8	Satisfaction with the extent of consultation by Supervisor concerning career aspirations and training needs
33	STRNG9	Satisfaction with the relevance of internal courses offered by the organisation
33	STRNG10	Satisfaction with equality of opportunity to access available training in the organisation
33	STRNG11	Satisfaction with the overall quality of training available in the organisation for my type of work
33	STRNG12	Satisfaction with study leave provisions in the organisation
33	STRNG13	Satisfaction with adequacy of training for promotion
34	CAREAD1	Importance of career development for long term satisfaction at work
35	CAREAD2	Adequacy of current level of training to undertake present responsibilities
36	CAREAD3	Importance of adequate training in determining promotion prospects
37	CAREAD4	Satisfaction with prospects for future career development in the organisation

Analysis of Work Measures

Rummel (1970 p.31) asserted that "factor analysis can transform data to a form required to meet the assumptions of other techniques. For example, regression analysis assumes that if tests of significance are to be applied to the regression coefficients, the predictor or regressor variables are statistically independent. If the predictor variables to be used are correlated, thus violating the assumption, factor analysis can be employed to reduce them to a smaller set of uncorrelated variables. This smaller set can then be employed in the regression anlysis with the knowledge that the variation in the original data has not been lost. Likewise, if there is an embarrassment of dependent variables, their number may be reduced through factor analysis".

Rummel went on to argue that for the researcher unable to manipulate variables experimentally, and who must deal with data derived from an actual social setting, factor analysis is a substitute for the laboratory. Factor analysis, he argued, permits the researcher to separate different sources of variation and to adequately control undesirable influences on the variables of concern.

It was beyond the scope of this study to obtain truly independent predictors of the variables of concern. Nevertheless, the richness of data available from a survey designed specifically to capture data relating to previously identified areas of real concern to the population in question permits the construction through factor analysis of at least quasi independent variables.

It will not be argued here that reliable causal relationships can be established from the present quasi independent variables. It was expected that results would at least suggest rational design criteria for true experimental procedures to test at least some elements of the causal structure of Job Burnout in large organisational settings.

Individual responses to each of the two groups of survey items were subjected to separate factor analyses using the SPSSX principal factoring procedure with varimax rotation (SPSS Inc. 1983). A separate factor analysis was conducted for those items relating to Opportunity for Personal Growth and Development on the job because previous research on the relationship between burnout and perceptions of future prospects for personal growth and development at work has been limited to the study of this relationship among human service workers. It was anticipated that a separate factor analysis of these items in the present sample of public corporate sector employees would yield one or more specific independent variables in the domain of satisfaction with future development prospects.

Factor items were conservatively determined by including only those which loaded higher than 0.40 on a single factor. The factor solutions for each of these groups of items are presented in Tables 4 and 5. Table 4 depicts the rotated factor solution for items relating to Supervision, Job Satisfaction, Goal Clarity and Feedback and Communication. Table 5 depicts that for the items relating to Opportunity for Personal Growth and Development on the Job.

Table 4
Rotated Factor Solution for 29 items from E.E.O. Survey
Questionnaire Relating to Supervision, Job Satisfaction,
Feedback and Communication

Factor/Items	FACTOR I	II	III	Communality
FACTOR I (CONFACI) Satisfaction with task related communication				
SUPERV2 - Satisfaction with the quality of supervision provided by your Supervisor	.83			.74
SUPERV1 - Satisfaction with the working relationship you have with you Supervisor	.79			.70
FEEDBK1 - Adequacy of your Supervisor's efforts to give constructive feedback about your work	.79			.65
SUPERV3 - Satisfaction with your Supervisor's ability to make fair and reasonable recommendations on your promotability based on your work performance	.78			.67
FEEDBK2 - Satisfaction with the feedback and recognition you receive from your Supervisor about your work	.69			.59
WKSITN - Adequacy of Supervisor's awareness of your current work situation	.68			.47
GRIEVE 10 - Expected adequacy of supervisors response in the event of a work related grievance	.67			.49

Table 4 (continued)

Factor/Items	FACTOR			Communality
	1	II	III	
TALK1 - Satisfaction with the effectiveness of communication about work related issues between staff and management in your area of work	.60			.56
CLTYGOAL - Adequacy of work related goal clarity	.57			.36
TYPEWK3 - Satisfaction with the amount of work expected of you by your Supervisor	.57			.45
FACTOR II (CONFAC 2) Overall Satisfaction in Present Position				
SUPER2 - The degree to which you fully understand the provisions of the Superannuation Scheme		.65		.43
SUPER1 - Adequacy of information provided about the Superannuation Scheme before you decided to join		.63		.41
TYPEWK2 - Extent to which you find your work interesting and absorbing		.59		.50
FEEL1 - Overall level of satisfaction with present job		.57		.50
CAREER1 - Satisfaction with availability of career guidance in the organisation		.42		.25
FACTOR III (CONFAC 3) Satisfaction with conditions of Employment				
MATSAT - Adequacy of maternity leave conditions			.72	.59

Table 4 (continued)

Factor/Items	FACTOR			Communality
	I	II	III	
PATSAT - Adequacy of paternity leave conditions			.72	.55
HOURS2 - Satisfaction with flexibility of working hours			.52	.35
HOURS1 - Satisfaction with hours worked			.51	.32
SETPRIOR - Satisfaction with ability to set own task priorities			.42	.27
Eigenvalues	8.44	2.03	1.83	
% of variance explained	29.1%	7.0%	6.3%	

Note: Item Factor Loadings of <.3 excluded

Unit weighted scores were calculated incorporating items with loadings of 0.40 or greater on each factor subscale. Unit weighted scores were used in preference to factor scores as their interpretation in terms of observed variables is more straight-forward for the present purpose. They were however quite highly correlated in some cases. Correlations between variables used in the analysis are reported in Table 13. These scores comprised part of the independent variable set in a multiple regression analysis: the dependent variables being unit weighted scores on each of the subscales of the M.J.B.I.

Table 5

Rotated Factor Solution for 21 items from E.E.O. Survey
Questionnaire Relating to Opportunities for Personal
Growth and Development on the Job (n = 719)

Factor/Items	FACTOR			Communality
	I	II	III	
FACTOR I (TRNGFAC1) _Satisfaction with Opportunity for Personal Growth and Career Development_				
STRNG5 – Satisfaction with prospects of receiving training to make progress in the organisation	.80			.65
STRNG7 – Satisfaction with information received concerning training available in the organisation	.79			.63
STRNG9 – Satisfaction with the relevance of internal training courses offered by the organisation	.77			.63
STRNG3 – Satisfaction with opportunity to develop skill by attendance at training courses	.76			.60
STRNG11 – Satisfaction with the overall quality of training available in the organisation for my type of work	.72			.56
STRNG13 – Satisfaction with adequacy of training for promotion	.72			.60

Table 5 (Continued)

Factor/Items	FACTOR			Communality
	I	II	III	
STRNG8 - Satisfaction with the extent of consultation by Supervisor concerning career aspirations and training needs	.71			.64
STRNG6 - Satisfaction with the quality of training courses attended in the organisation	.69			.47
STRNG4 - Satisfaction with Supervisor's effort to ensure adequate training for the job	.63			.57
STRNG2 - Satisfaction with adequacy of "on the job" training received	.61			.45
TRNGNEED - Extent to which training needs have been considered by Supervisor	.57			.48
TRNGKNOW - Extent of knowledge of training programs offered by the organisation	.54			.41
STRNG12 - Satisfaction with the study leave provisions of the organisation	.48			.24
FACTOR II (TRNGFAC2) Satisfaction with Organisational Support for Career Development				
SUPERPRO2 - Satisfaction with encouragement received from Supervisor to apply for promotion		.78		.65
SUPERPRO1 - Extent of Supervisor's encouragement to apply for promotion in the organisation		.72		.60
CAREAD4 - Satisfaction with prospects for future career development in the organisation	.33	.52		.41

Table 5 (Continued)

Factor/Items	I	FACTOR II	III	Communality
FACTOR III (TRNGFAC3) Need for Personal Growth and Development on the Job				
CAREAD1 - Importance of career development for long term satisfaction at work			.72	.54
CAREAD3 - Importance of adequate training in determining promotion prospects			.56	.33
Eigenvalues	7.61	1.55	1.26	
% of variance explained	36.3%	7.4%	6.0%	

Note: Item Factor Loadings of <.3 excluded

Data Analysis

Analysis of the Modified Job Burnout Inventory

Data from all completed Modified Job Burnout Inventories was subjected to factor analysis using the SPSSX principal factoring procedure with varimax rotation (SPSSX Inc. 1983).

Factor items were then determined using the same criteria as those applied by Ford et al. (1983): a factor loading greater than 0.35 on only one of the resulting factors. Factors were extracted with eigenvalues greater than 1.0.

Separate identical factor analyses were conducted for males and females in the sample. The robustness of the factor solution was demonstrated since all items in the separate factor solutions loaded on the same factors as those derived from the total sample.

Unit weighted scores were calculated incorporating items loading 0.35 or greater on each factor subscale. These factor scores were used as the dependent variables in a multiple regression analysis details of which follow.

Analysis of Relationships Between the Subscales of the
M.J.B.I. Demographic and Work Measures

Relationships between scores on the three factor subscales of the M.J.B.I., the dependent variables, and the following independent variables were examined by means of SPSSX stepwise regression analysis. Draper and Smith (1966 p.171), recommend the method of stepwise regression, since it constitutes an improvement on the forward selection procedure.

Two categories of independent variables were included in the regression analysis. The first was sociodemographic variables, including age, gender, marital status, education level, salary and whether or not the respondent was a wages or salaried employee.

Research questions concerning burnout among the demographic subgroupings of interest in the present study have been prompted by the results of previous burnout research among human service workers. The burnout literature is equivocal concerning the incidence of burnout among several of the sociodemographic subgroups of present research interest.

Owing to the limited sample size of corporate sector employees in their study Ford et al. (1983) were unable to present an analysis of the J.B.I. for any demographic subgroups. The sample of both sexes used in the present study was considered adequate to permit analysis of the identified subscales of the M.J.B.I. for the selected demographic subgroups in the organisation.

The second category comprised the six work scales derived from the factor analyses of 50 items from the E.E.O. survey questionnaire. These six derived measures were:

(a)   CONFAC1 - Satisfaction with task related communication

(b)   CONFAC2 - Overall satisfaction with present position

(c)   CONFAC3 - Satisfaction with conditions of employment

(d)   TRNGFAC1 - Satisfaction with opportunity for personal growth

        and career development

(e)   TRNGFAC2 - Satisfaction with organisation support for career

        development

(f)   TRNGFAC3 - Need for personal growth and development on the job.

Results

The Modified Job Burnout Inventory

The factor solution for the total sample is presented in Table 6. Two items which loaded higher than 0.35 on more than one factor were eliminated from the factor solution (Items 6 and 11).

The remaining 14 items entered into three factor subscales which were labelled:

I. Frustration, Exhaustion and Defeat which describes feelings of being frustrated, helpless, out of options, isolated, exhausted and defeated (Items 9, 15, 2, 13, 7, 4 and 16).

II. Resource Inadequacy which describes feelings of strain arising from the belief that available resources are insufficient to cope adequately with personal matters as well as having to respond to conflicting job demands (Items 14, 8, 10 and 12).

III. Lowered Self Efficacy which describes feelings of low self confidence and inadequate coping at work (Items 5, 1 and 3).

Item loadings provided strong support for the conceptual independence of the factor scales.

Table 6

Rotated Factor Matrix for Modified Job Burnout Inventory
(n = 703)

Factor/Items	FACTOR			Communality
	I	II	III	
I Frustration, Exhaustion and Defeat Scale				
9 I feel frustrated by my job	.75			.59
15 My job is such that I can effect little change in the work situation	.68			.47
2 No matter what I do things at work don't seem to get better	.66			.46
13 I feel unable to express and share dissatisfaction about my job	.63	.33		.51
7 I feel a sense of isolation from the rest of my peers, co-workers, etc.	.61			.41
4 I feel used up at the end of the work day	.56	.31		.38
16 Temporarily removing myself from the job environment seems to resolve my feelings	.47			.27
II Resource Inadequacy Scale				
14 My work load is impossible to catch up		.75		.59

Table 6 (continued)

Factor/Items	FACTOR I	II	III	Communality
8 I generally have sufficient time or resources to do my job (Reverse Scored)		.68		.55
10 I experience conflicting demands in my job		.61		.50
12 I have difficulty attending to family or personal needs		.60		.41
III Lowered Self Efficacy Scale				
5 I feel confident about the quality of any work (Reverse Scored)			.75	.56
1 I cope well with the pressure of my work (Reverse Scored)			.73	.60
3 I cope well with uncertainty at work (Reverse Scored)			.66	.45
Eigenvalues	4.67	1.87	1.30	
% of variance explained	29.1%	11.5%	8.1%	

Note: Item Factor Loadings of <.3 excluded

Twenty-four male participants and four females submitted incomplete Modified Job Burnout Inventories or omitted this section of the questionnaire altogether. Data from incomplete Modified Job Burnout Inventories was omitted from the analysis.

Table 7 presents descriptive statistics for each of the subscales of the Modified Job Burnout Inventory by sex.

Table 7

Descriptive Statistics for the Three Modified Job Burnout
Inventory Subscales: Results are presented separately
for each sex

Samples	n	I Frustration, Exhaustion & Defeat		II Resource Inadequacy		III Lowered Self Efficacy	
		M	SD	M	SD	M	SD
Sex							
Male	442	19.44	5.84	10.32	3.33	6.94	2.25
Female	261	19.77	5.98	9.09	3.17	7.12	2.45
Age							
Male							
-30	116	19.12	5.78	9.55	3.10	7.39	2.41
30-49	250	20.23	6.08	10.56	3.41	6.89	2.24
50+	76	18.96	5.86	9.87	3.56	6.46	2.31
Females							
-30	141	20.24	6.14	9.35	3.40	7.48	2.42
30-49	85	19.23	5.80	9.27	3.02	6.94	2.46
50+	27	19.84	5.99	8.71	3.26	6.29	2.67
Marital Status							
Male							
Single	80	20.18	6.13	9.78	3.41	7.42	2.38
Married	328	19.01	5.70	10.39	3.29	6.82	2.10
Divorced	22	21.49	5.94	11.20	3.63	6.89	2.24
Other	10	23.14	6.16	10.60	3.51	7.04	2.30
Females							
Single	97	19.90	6.06	8.65	3.32	7.42	2.39
Married	122	19.16	5.91	9.04	3.14	6.78	2.58
Divorced	22	21.86	6.12	9.63	3.28	7.71	2.01
Other	14	20.97	5.99	9.79	3.01	6.87	1.99

Table 7 (continued)

Samples	n	M	SD	M	SD	M	SD
Education							
Males							
No tertiary Qualification	284	19.42	5.68	9.77	3.52	6.91	2.42
Tertiary & Post Graduate	150	19.48	6.12	10.81	3.21	7.00	2.19
Females							
No tertiary Qualification	202	19.50	5.74	8.96	3.22	7.08	2.68
Tertiary & Post Graduate	52	20.81	6.32	9.61	3.02	7.27	2.47
Salary							
Males							
- $20,500	143	19.27	5.82	10.40	3.41	6.99	2.24
$20,500 to $26,500	143	18.52	5.72	10.52	3.46	7.07	2.31
+ $26,500	157	19.63	5.84	11.59	3.62	6.95	2.21
Females							
- $17,500	99	19.90	5.98	8.67	3.18	7.03	2.44
$17,500 to $20,500	84	20.21	6.02	9.44	3.41	7.24	2.37
+ $20,500	74	19.80	6.07	9.84	3.52	7.18	2.42

Demographic Data

In general, males scored significantly higher than females on the Resource Inadequacy Subscale of the M.J.B.I., particularly in the 30 - 49 age group $F(1,701) = 17,64$ p < .01.

Patterns of Burnout varied by age differently for each sex. Males aged between 30-49 scored significantly higher than other age groups on the subscale Resource Inadequacy $F(2,439) = 5.86$ p<.01.

Younger groups of males and females are each significantly more likely to score higher on the subscale Lowered Self Efficacy. The tendency was observed to be more marked for females however. $F(2,258) = 6.04$ p<.01, compared to $F(2,439) = 3.74$ p<.05. for males.

Marital status among females was significantly related to scores on the Lowered Self-Efficacy scale. Lower scores on this scale observed among married women compared to single and divorced women, $F(3,258) = 4.58$ p<.05, must be treated with caution since marital status is confounded with age in the sample.

Differences by level of education were observed only on the Resource Inadequacy Subscale of the M.J.B.I. Tertiary education among males was significantly related to higher scores on this factor $F(1,440) = 7.66$ p<.01. The same trend was apparent among females but failed to reach statistical significance at the 0.__ level $F(1,259) = 2.78$ p=.1. This may be due to the relatively small proportion of females in the sample with tertiary level education.

Salary level was significantly related to Resource Inadequacy but not to either of the other M.J.B.I. subscales. Among males greater levels of income were associated with higher scores on this subscale $F(2,439) = 6.01$ p<.01. Higher salaries among females were also associated with elevated scores on the Resource Inadequacy subscale $F(2,258) = 4.89$ p<.05.

Relationship Between the Subscales of M.J.B.I. and Selected Work
Measures

Work Satisfaction Items

Correlations between the subscales of the M.J.B.I. and work
satisfaction items analogous to those reported by Ford et al. (1983)
are depicted in Table 8. Significant negative correlations between
each of these items and Frustration, Exhaustion and Defeat, the first
subscale of the M.J.B.I. are almost identical with those reported by
Ford et al. (1983) for the first subscale of burnout on their J.B.I.,
Emotional Exhaustion and Defeat, among private sector corporate
employees. Ford et al. (1983) reported a significant negative
correlation between Resource Inadequacy and satisfaction with
supervision. Similar significant correlations were also found in this
study for males and females with a single exception. The correlation
between Resource Inadequacy and satisfaction with working relationship
with Supervisor failed to reach statistical significance for females.

For both sexes the negative correlation between the Resource
Inadequacy subscale and satisfaction with the amount of work expected
by the Supervisor were markedly higher than for other aspects of
satisfaction with supervision.

Among males, a negative correlation between the Resource
Inadequacy subscale and satisfaction with type of work achieved
significance; for females this correlation although negative, was not
significant. This result may well reflect the significantly higher
ratio of males to female subjects in the present study compared to
that of Ford et al. (1983).

Table 8

Correlations of M.J.B.I. Subscales with Selected Work
Satisfaction Items from E.E.O. Questionnaire

Item No.	Item Content	I Frustration Exhaustion & Defeat		II Resource Inadequacy		III Lowered Self Efficacy	
		M	F	M	F	M	F
Q46:	Satisfaction with type of work	*** -.38	*** -.45	* -.08	-.04	*** -.16	-.07
Q46:	Satisfaction with amount of work expected by your Supervisor	*** -.39	*** -.41	*** -.28	*** -.30	-.06	-.09
Q46:	Satisfaction with your working relationship with your Supervisor	*** -.37	*** -.34	** -.13	-.07	-.07	+.05
Q46:	Satisfaction with quality of supervision	*** -.39	*** -.38	*** -.15	** -.14	-.01	+.05
Q46:	Satisfaction with Supervisor's recommendations on promotion	*** -.43	*** -.42	*** -.18	*** -.19	.01	+.05
Q46:	Satisfaction with pay	** -.23	*** -.28	** -.14	* -.11	+.01	** +.16
Q23:	Satisfaction with future prospects	*** -.36	*** -.50	** -.11	** -.13	* -.08	* -.11
Q48:	Satisfaction with goal clarity	*** -.30	*** -.37	*** -.16	*** -.22	-.06	.00
Q51:	Satisfaction with feedback on performance	*** -.40	*** -.57	*** -.17	*** -.23	.00	-.08

N FOR MALES   = 442   Note: Two tailed tests * p .05
N FOR FEMALES = 261   ** p .01
                                                    *** p .001

None of the correlations between Lowered Self Efficacy and satisfaction with supervision achieved statistical significance for either sex. There were non significant positive correlations for females between this subscale and three of the four measures of satisfaction with supervision. This result suggests that less confident females may be marginally more tolerant of the supervision they receive from predominantly male supervisors.

A statistically significant negative correlation was apparent for both sexes between the two subscales of Frustration, Exhaustion and Defeat and Resource Inadequacy and satisfaction with pay.

A significant positive correlation was found among females between satisfaction with pay and lowered self efficacy. This result suggests that women with less confidence at work are more satisfied with their pay than women with higher expectations of self efficacy. The relationship between these two variables for males failed to achieve statistical significance.

Significant negative correlations emerged for both sexes between all three subscales of the M.J.B.I. and satisfaction with future prospects. The negative relationship between the Lowered Self Efficacy subscale of M.J.B.I. and satisfaction with future prospects was the only correlation to achieve statistical significance for both sexes. Significant negative correlations were found between the first two subscales of burnout for both sexes and satisfaction with goal clarity and feedback on performance.

Disability

Forty-nine males reported suffering "other disabilities including chronic illness/pain". These males were significantly more likely to score high on the first subscale of burnout, Frustration, Exhaustion and Defeat if they reported their disability as severe or moderate $F(2,46) = 8.08$ $p < .01$. A similar relationship was found for the scores of these subjects on the second subscale of burnout Resource Inadequacy $F(2,46) = 3.69$ $p < .05$.

Work Locations

The only significant difference in burnout subscale scores apparent between geographic work locations was among males on the second Burnout subscale Resource Inadequacy $F(17,424) = 1.84$ $p < .05$.

It is interesting to note that four of the five locations with highest average scores among males on this subscale have been engaged for some time in new road or freeway construction. The fifth location, an established facility, was undergoing major organisational change.

Occupational Type

Differences by occupational type were found for males and females on the first two subscales of the Modified Job Burnout Inventory.

Mean scores on the subscale Frustration, Exhaustion and Defeat
for males and females in each occupational group appear in Table 9.

Table 9

M.J.B.I. Subscale I: Frustration, Exhaustion and Defeat.
Mean Score for each Occupational Group

Occupational Group	Males (N) mean score	Females (N) mean score
Management and Supervision	24.42 (23)	-
Non Engineering Professionals	24.11 (21)	29.63 (11)
Secretaries	-	23.83 (14)
Survey Officers	20.43 (28)	-
Scientists and Technicians	19.73 (45)	21.13 (24)
Engineers	19.63 (98)	19.73 (7)
Road Building Personnel	19.13 (87)	-
Administrative & Clerical Officers	19.00 (60)	20.54 (84)
Drafting Officers	16.83 (56)	18.83 (34)
Typist/Word Processor Operators	-	17.83 (68)
Other Female Groups (Catering, Gardening, etc.)	-	16.81 (19)
Drivers/Storemen/Maintenance	16.53 (24)	-

Differences between mean scores for male and female occupational
groups covered a similar range. For both sexes the differences were
significant at $p<.05$ Males: $F(8,433) = 2.17$ and Females: $F(7,253) = 2.24$.

Mean scores for males and females from each occupational group on the subscale Resource Inadequacy appear in Table 10. For both sexes the differences were significant at p<.01 Males: $F(8,433) = 5.15$ and Females: $F(7,253) = 5.32$.

Table 10

M.J.B.I. Subscale II: Resource Inadequacy
Mean Score for each Occupational Group

Occupational Group	Males (N) mean score	Females (N) mean score
Engineers	11.29 (98)	9.60 (7)
Non Engineering Professionals	11.27 (21)	11.00 (11)
Survey Officers	10.78 (28)	-
Management and Supervision	10.60 (23)	-
Administrative & Clerical Officers	10.26 (60)	9.02 (84)
Road Building Personnel	10.08 (87)	-
Scientists and Technicians	9.98 (45)	9.60 (24)
Drafting Officers	9.18 (56)	9.26 (34)
Drivers/Storeman/Maintenance	8.88 (24)	-
Secretaries	-	10.90 (14)
Typist/Word Processor Operators	-	8.42 (68)
Other Female Groups (Catering, Gardening, etc.)	-	8.45 (19)

Mean scores for males and females from each occupational group on the subscale Lowered Self Efficacy appear in Table 11. Differences between mean scores failed to reach statistical significance for either sex (Males: $F(9,432) = 1.38$ Females: $F(8,252) = 1.04$).

Table 11

M.J.B.I. Subscale III: Lowered Self Efficacy
Mean Score for each Occupational Group

Occupational Group	Males (N) mean score	Females (N) mean score
Non Engineering Professionals	7.5 (21)	7.3 (11)
Administrative Officers	7.4 (43)	6.9 (34)
Engineers	7.2 (98)	6.3 (7)
Drafting Officers	7.1 (56)	7.5 (34)
Survey Officers	7.0 (28)	-
Scientists and Technicians	6.9 (45)	7.6 (24)
Road Building Personnel	6.8 (87)	-
Driver/Storeman/Maintenance	6.8 (24)	-
Management and Supervision	6.6 (23)	-
Clerical Officers	6.4 (17)	7.0 (50)
Secretaries	-	7.4 (14)
Typist/Word Processor Operators	-	6.9 (68)
Other Female Groups (Catering, Gardening, etc.)	-	7.1 (19)

Correlation Between Variables used in the Regression Analysis

Correlations among the dependent and independent variables used in a stepwise multiple regression analysis are reported in Table 12. The results summarized in Table 12 indicate that the variables having the strongest zero order relationship to Frustration, Exhaustion and Defeat are CONFAC1: Task Related Communication (r = -.48), CONFAC2: Overall Job Satisfaction (r = -.30) and TRNGFAC1: Opportunity for Career Development (r = -.26).

Variables having the strongest zero order relationship to Resource Inadequacy are Salary Level (r = .28), CONFAC1: Task Related Communication (r = -.21), Education Level (r = .11) and CONFAC2: Overall Job Satisfaction (r = .11).

Variables having the strongest zero order relationship to Lowered Self Efficacy are Age (r = - .20), Marital Status (r = -.15) and CONFAC2: Overall Job Satisfaction (r = -.11).

The Regression Analysis

The results of a forward stepwise multiple regression analysis for predictors of identified subscales of burnout for each sex are presented in Table 13. Separate regression analyses were conducted for each sex because of the different sampling schedule used for each.

Table 12: Means, Standard Deviations and Correlations Between Dependent and Independent Variables

VARIABLE	M	S.D.	1	2	3	4	5	6	7	8	9	10	11	12	13	14
Dependent Variables: Subscales of Job Burnout																
1 Frustration, Exhaustion and Defeat (FAC1)	19.59	6.07														
2 Resource Inadequacy (FAC2)	9.88	3.42	.52													
3[d] Lowered Self Efficacy at Work (FAC3)	7.01	2.36	.19	.24												
Independent Variables																
4 Adequacy of Task Related Communication (CONFAC1)	48.40	10.61	-.48	-.21	-.02											
5 Overall Job Satisfaction (CONFAC2)	23.76	4.37	-.30	-.11	-.10	.32										
6 Conditions of Employment (CONFAC3)	32.74	7.96	-.02	-.07	-.02	.06	.16									
7 Opportunity for Personal Growth and Career Development (TRNGFAC1)	44.10	10.05	-.26	-.08	-.07	.35	.19	.05								
8 Organisational Support for Training and Development (TRNGFAC2)	11.10	3.60	.15	.08	.06	-.24	-.09	-.02	-.13							
9 Need for Personal Growth and Career Development (TRNGFAC3)	4.86	1.34	-.02	.04	.01	.03	-.04	.00	.01	-.02						
10 Age	34.44	10.81	-.02	.05	-.20	.05	.22	-.04	.03	-.19	-.03					
11 Sex (1 = male/2 = female)	1.56	0.50	.05	-.17	.05	-.14	-.11	.06	-.19	.05	-.10	-.25				
12 Marital (1 = single/2 = married)	1.57	0.50	-.04	.04	-.15	.02	.07	.04	.06	-.06	.04	.37	-.29			
13[b] Education Level	5.83	2.66	.01	.11	.05	.07	.06	-.01	.17	.03	.13	-.15	-.21	-.02		
14 Salary	$21.32k	$6.87k	.01	.28	-.04	.09	.14	.10	.24	-.03	.06	.27	-.42	.26	.57	
15 Wages or Salaried Staff (2 = wages/1 = salaried)	1.20	.38	.05	-.04	-.05	-.08	-.01	-.01	-.12	-.04	-.03	-.08	-.21	-.01	-.40	-.40

NOTE: Number of observations was 733 (468m - 265f)
Correlations above .06 and .09 are significant at p .05 and .01 respectively

a - the higher the response, the less the individual feels self Efficacy at Work

b - categories for education were as follows: 3 = Form 4 or less 4 = Form 5 5 = HSC 6 = Apprenticeship
7 = Certificate 8 = Diploma 9 = University Degree 10 = Postgraduate Degree

Table 13

Forward Stepwise Multiple Regression Analysis for
Predictors of Identified Subscales of M.J.B.I.
(Results are presented for each sex separately)

Males			Females		
Step	Independent Variables		Step	Independent Variables	

M.J.B.I. Subscale 1 : FRUSTRATION, EXHAUSTION AND DEFEAT

		BETA			BETA
1.	Adequacy of Task Related Communication (CONFAC1)	*** -.48	1.	Adequacy of Task Related Communication (CONFAC1)	*** -.52
2.	Overall Satisfaction in Present Position (CONFAC2)	*** -.17	2.	Overall Satisfaction in Present Position (CONFAC2)	*** -.18
3.	Opportunity for Personal Growth & Career Development (TRNGFAC1)	* -.11			
4.	Salary	* +.09			
	$R^2 = .27$			$R^2 = .30$	

M.J.B.I. Subscale II: Resource Inadequacy

1.	Salary	*** .29	1.	Adequacy of Task Related Communication (CONFAC1)	*** -.22
2.	Adequacy of Task Related Communication (CONFAC1)	*** -.24	2.	Salary	** .19
			3.	Age	* -.14
	$R^2 = .14$			$R^2 = .10$	

M.J.B.I. Subscale III: Lowered Self Efficacy

1.	Age	*** -.17	1.	Age	*** -.26
2.	Wages or Salaried Staff (OFFRTYPL)	* -.09	2.	Marital Status	* -.13
	$R^2 = .04$			$R^2 = .08$	

***	$p<.001$	Note:	Variables included if they added
**	$p<.01$		to the prediction of the
*	$p<.05$		dependent variable at a significance
			level of .05.

M.J.B.I. Subscale I: Frustration, Exhaustion and Defeat

The regression analyses revealed that only CONFAC1 - Adequacy of Task Related Communication and CONFAC2 - Overall Satisfaction in Present Position, significantly predicted M.J.B.I. Subscale I, Frustration, Exhaustion and Defeat for both males and females.

Those employees of both sexes who reported lower levels of satisfaction with the adequacy of task related communication in the organisation, and whose overall level of job satisfaction in their present position was also lower, obtained higher scores on the first subscale of the M.J.B.I., Frustration, Exhaustion and Defeat.

TRNGFAC1 - Opportunity for Personal Growth and Career Development and Salary level also added significantly to prediction of scores on this subscale for males. Those males on higher salaries who were less satisfied with opportunity for Personal Growth and Career Development reported higher levels of Frustration, Exhaustion and Defeat.

M.J.B.I. Subscale II: Resource Inadequacy

CONFAC1 - Adequacy of Task Related Communication and Salary level were included as significant predictors of the Resource Inadequacy subscale of the M.J.B.I. for both sexes. For females, a smaller proportion of variance was explained by these variables, and in particular, salary appears to play a smaller predictive role for females. It is noteworthy that a higher salary level is associated with higher scores on the Resource Inadequacy Subscale for both sexes.

Among females, Age also adds to the regression equation, with younger females perceiving greater Resource Inadequacy.

M.J.B.I. Subscale III: Lowered Self Efficacy

Age was a significant predictor of Lowered Self Efficacy for both sexes : the scores of younger employees reflecting lower expectations for Self Efficacy at work. Among males Salaried Status in the organisation was a significant predictor of scores on this subscale : Salaried males reporting lower Self Efficacy expectations at work than those in wages work. For females, Marital Status added significantly to the regression equation : single, divorced or separated women reporting lower Self Efficacy at work than their married colleagues.

Discussion

The Modified Job Burnout Inventory

Ford, Murphy and Edwards (1983) developed a Job Burnout Inventory and obtained different factor solutions for corporate sector employees than obtained for human service workers. The first two subscales of the M.J.B.I. derived from the present sample of public sector corporate employees is substantially the same as the forced two factor solution reported by Ford et al. (1983) for private sector corporate employees. This lends only a modicum of support however to their assertion that corporate sector employees process information about stressful job conditions in different ways to human service workers. This assertion must remain speculative for two reasons. First, present results suggest that human service workers and corporate sector employees are likely to share many, if not most, of the feelings reportedly associated with burnout. Second, the percentage of total variance explained by the second subscale of the M.J.B.I., that upon which Ford et al. (1983) asserted human service workers and corporate sector employees differ in their experience of burnout, was less than half of that reported by those authors.

The family of feelings akin to emotional exhaustion has consistently emerged as the principal component of burnout among a wide range of human service workers and teachers. Frustration, Exhaustion and Defeat, the principal subscale derived from responses to the M.J.B.I. accounts for less than 30% of total variance among public sector corporate employees in the present study. 14 of the 16 items in the M.J.B.I. are included in the three subscales identified. Together these subscales account for less than 50% of total variance which is markedly less than the 78% reported by Ford et al. (1983) for the forced two factor solution of the Job Burnout Inventory among corporate sector employees in their sample.

Substantial similarities exist in the make up of the principal factor subscale of the M.J.B.I. when it is compared with that obtained from both the Maslach Burnout Inventory and the first subscale of the J.B.I. in a forced two factor solution. Notwithstanding this similarity in the first subscale the three subscales identified in the present sample account for a notably smaller proportion of total variance than those identified by either Maslach and Jackson (1981) or Ford et al. (1983).

The present data suggest that while human service employees may process information about stressful job conditions somewhat differently to those in the corporate sector they share many similar feelings of emotional exhaustion, frustration and defeat supposed to constitute the principal component of the burnout construct.

The second subscale of the M.J.B.I. identified in the present study, Resource Inadequacy, comprised four items. Three of these items were identical to those reported by Ford et al. (1983) and loaded in the same order on the scale. The first item of this subscale in the present study, "My work load is impossible to catch up" (Item 14 on the M.J.B.I.) was dropped from the inventory developed by Ford et al. (1983) because it loaded as a single item factor. The first item of Ford et al.'s Resource Inadequacy subscale, "My work is characterized by intense pressure and deadlines on the job" was not included in the M.J.B.I. because it was objectionable to the senior management group in the organisation. In view of the semantic similarity of the item dropped from the J.B.I. by Ford et al. (1983), which appeared in the second subscale of the M.J.B.I., and the item dropped from the present item pool because it was unacceptable, the same title as that given by Ford et al. (1983), Resource Inadequacy was used for the second subscale of the M.J.B.I.

The third subscale of the M.J.B.I. is comprised of the three items which were included in the inventory to measure expectations of self efficacy and personal accomplishment. Since Meier (1983) postulated that low self efficacy expectations directly influence the subjective experience of burnout this subscale was named the lowered Self Efficacy Scale. Appearance of this group of items as a separate factor subscale of the M.J.B.I. provides some support as follows for the work of Maslach and Jackson (1981), Ford et al. (1983) and Meier (1983). Maslach and Jackson (1981) reported a subscale of burnout which they called the Personal Accomplishment scale. This scale described self reported feelings of efficacy at work among human service workers. Items comprising the scale were reverse scored on the Maslach Burnout Inventory : in this manner low expectations for self efficacy at work comprised a scale of burnout on the M.B.I. The present results thus tend to support the findings of Maslach and Jackson (1981) in a corporate sector sample.

The Job Burnout Inventory (J.B.I.) developed by Ford et al. (1983) was designed to measure two aspects of burnout which they hypothesized to be common to both human service workers and corporate sector employees. These were emotional exhaustion and feelings of demoralisation and reduced efficiency. Present results suggest the subscales of burnout identified by Ford et al. (1983) among corporate sector employees to be independent of the Personal Accomplishment scale identified by Maslach and Jackson (1981).

The model of burnout proposed by Meier (1983) suggested that expectations of low self efficacy at work lead to overgeneralisation errors and thus burnout. Scores on the third subscale comprising the M.J.B.I., Lowered Self Efficacy, and the relationship of this subscale to the first two subscales indicate that expectations of lowered self efficacy and personal accomplishment at work are significantly related in the present sample to the first two subscales of the M.J.B.I., each of which has been claimed by Ford et al. (1983) to be a component of burnout among corporate sector employees.

Results reported here suggest that expectations of diminished personal accomplishment, as meaured by the Lowered Self Efficacy subscale of the M.J.B.I., may be as potentially important a component of burnout among corporate sector employees as Maslach and Jackson

(1981) found them to be among human service workers. This conjecture is based on the observation, though not statistically significant, of what appears to be a potentially significant trend for scores to vary according to the demand characteristics and level of task role uncertainty of different occupations depicted in Table 11. For this reason it is felt that any future inventory designed to measure burnout among corporate sector employees should include a broader range of items to measure expectations of self efficacy and personal accomplishment at work.

Present results are consistent with those reported by Stevens and O'Neil (1983) on the relationship between burnout and expectations for self efficacy at work among human service workers. Lower expectations for self efficacy at work among the present sample of public sector corporate employees are significantly associated with higher scores on each of the other two subscales of the M.J.B.I. This result supports the general predictions of the model of burnout proposed by Meier (1983) and suggests that a similar but more modest relationship exists between burnout and expectations for self efficacy at work among public sector corporate employees than that reported among the human service workers studied by Stevens and O'Neil (1983). Although statistically significant at the $p < .01$ level, each of the above correlations is quite small, accounting for less than 5% of variance.

In a multiple regression analysis the present measure of lowered self efficacy narrowly failed to predict a significant

proportion of variance in either of the other two subscales of the
M.J.B.I. This suggests that either the present measure of expected
self efficacy was inadequate or that expectations of low self efficacy
at work may not be a critical component in the explanatory model of
burnout proposed by Meier (1983). An alternative explanation,
assuming the M.J.B.I. provides a useful measure of burnout, may be that
self efficacy expectations in the present sample of public sector
corporate employees are outweighed by more powerfully correlated
organisational determinants of burnout. The correlations reported
here between the first two subscales of the M.J.B.I., supposed by Ford
et al. (1983) to reliably measure burnout among corporate sector
employees, and expectations of diminished personal accomplishment, as
measured by the Lowered Self Efficacy subscale of the M.J.B.I., while
statistically significant as would have been predicted by Pines,
Aronson and Kafry (1981) are not powerfully supportive of either of
the models of burnout proposed by Golembiewski et al. (1983) or Meier
(1983).

Tentative general support was provided by the present results
for the stage model of burnout proposed by Golembiewski et al. (1983)
based on the assumption that the Resource Inadequacy Subscale of the
M.J.B.I. is a component of burnout among corporate sector employees.
If not a component of burnout at least an indicator of diminished
personal accomplishment. In the model proposed by Golembiewski et al.
(1983) Emotional Exhaustion is the final stage in burnout, and is
preceded by diminished personal accomplishment. The significantly
higher scores on the Resource Inadequacy subscale of the M.J.B.I. at

some work locations, in the absence of similiarity elevated scores on Frustration, Exhaustion and Defeat, suggests that the role overload described by the former of these subscales precedes Frustration, Exhaustion and Defeat in the development of burnout. This assertion is based on the assumption that if Frustration, Exhaustion and Defeat preceded, or is concomitant with Resource Inadequacy, higher scores on that subscale would be expected at those locations in which subscale scores on the Resource Inadequacy component of burnout were found to be significantly higher. Significantly higher scores on Frustration Exhaustion and Defeat were not apparent at those locations.

Correlations of the magnitude reported here suggest that any satisfactorily predictive stage model of burnout will demand a great deal more in its formulation and later confirmation than cross sectional data.

Ford et al. (1983) developed the J.B.I. in anticipation of its usefulness as a more universal brief measure of burnout than had up to that time been available. Present results using a M.J.B.I. suggest that burnout, at least among public sector corporate employees, constitutes a multifactorial phenomenon to a greater extent than was reflected in the results reported by Ford et al. (1983).

The first two subscales of the factor solution reported for the M.J.B.I. in the present heterogeneous sample of public sector corporate employees closely approximate those reported by Ford et al. (1983) for private sector corporate employees. This result is supportive of the usefulness of each inventory to measure some of the important hypothesized components of the burnout construct among a wide range of corporate sector employees. The case for considering the principal subscale of the M.J.B.I., Frustration, Exhaustion and Defeat, a component of burnout is stronger for two reasons than that for including the second subscale, Resource Inadequacy,. First, the domain of the item content of the subscale is similar to that comprising the Emotional Exhaustion subscale of the Maslach Burnout Inventory and reflects similar feeling states. Second, the items included in the Resource Inadequacy subscale are dissimilar to any previously reported in the burnout literature, and more importantly, do not describe feeling states. Each of them can be described instead as suggesting a possible reason for these feeling states. The R.I. subscale can thus be described as a scale of attribution, potentially useful in burnout research, but perhaps not a component of burnout itself.

Addition of three items to the Ford et al. (1983) J.B.I. hypothesized to be capable of measuring expectations of self efficacy at work proved to be justified as these items were all included in a separate factor subscale. Items in this subscale are analogous to those comprising the Personal Accomplishment subscale of burnout reported by Maslach and Jackson (1981). Expectations of diminished personal accomplishment have thus been tentatively demonstrated by the present results to play a possible common role in the burnout phenomenon among human service workers and public sector corporate employees. Inclusion of all three items in a separate subscale of the

M.J.B.I. among corporate sector employees suggests the possibility
that further extension and refinement of the Lowered Self Efficacy
subscale may facilitate greater understanding of the burnout construct
among corporate sector employees. Expectations of lowered self
efficacy and personal accomplishment have been hypothesized by Pines
et al. (1981), Golembiewski et al. (1983) and Meier (1983) to play an
important, though as yet incompletely defined, role in the development
of burnout. Present results suggest that this role is deserving of
further exploration. A clearer understanding of the relationship
between expectations of self efficacy and the manifestations of
burnout may be a necessary prerequisite for development of any
effective strategy for prevention and management of burnout phenomena
and perhaps other forms of dysfunctional occupational stress.

The Regression Analysis

Significant predictive correlates of each of the subscales of
the M.J.B.I. reported in a multiple regression analysis are discussed
here for each subscale separately and the discussion is amplified in
later sections where these correlates have relevance to other
significant results.

The most powerful predictive correlate of the first subscale of
the M.J.B.I., Frustration, Exhaustion and Defeat, for both sexes was
CONFAC1, Adequacy of Task Related Communication. This variable
strongly reflects the perceived quality of the communication process
between the employee and his or her supervisor. This result suggests

that the task structuring component of the interpersonal relationship
between employees and their supervisors is the most influential
determinant of the feelings reflected in the first subscale of the
M.J.B.I. Item factor loadings on the independent variable CONFAC1 in
the regression analysis provide support for Snyder and Morris (1984)
conclusion that performance feedback is of the greatest importance for
individual feelings of self efficacy at work among public sector
corporate employees.

The relationship reported by Keenan and Newton (1985) between
inadequate task related communication and the affective response of
frustration and anger among engineers is also reflected in this
result. Item loadings on the subscale Frustration, Exhaustion and
Defeat, strongly suggest that feelings of frustration and anger are
predominant among those with higher scores on this subscale of the
M.J.B.I. It would seem likely that efforts by supervisors to limit
role ambiguity in the organisation might well have significant strain
reducing effects as concluded by Ford et al. (1983).

Maslach and Jackson (1981) concluded that employees
experiencing emotional exhaustion are unaware of their own level of
effectiveness and resistant to attempts made to change those features
of the organisation perceived to have brought about these feelings in
the first place. This assertion is consistent with that of
Golembiewski et al. (1983); namely that the level of stimulus load is
already perceived to be close to the limits of tolerance among those
experiencing emotional exhaustion. Invocations of the type proposed

by Pines et al. (1981) for these employees to adopt a positive attitude and active coping strategy concomitant with the experience of such feelings seems destined to meet with greater resistance. Ganster et al. (1983) argued that no solution is likely to be effective that does not consider both the position of the individual and the demands made upon that person by the organisation. Sharit and Salvendy (1982) have asserted that the degree of fit between individual and the organisation determines the experience of dysfunctional stress and strain. Individuals experiencing Frustration, Exhaustion and Defeat in the present corporate sector environment perceive their supervisors as capable of making some beneficial changes in this fit by greater efforts to improve task related communication.

Component items in the predictor scale CONFAC1 are consistent with those reported by Berkeley Planning Associates (1977) suggesting that in several important respects human service workers and corporate sector employees make similar attributions concerning the origins of negative feelings associated with burnout.

Items comprising the task related communication scale (CONFAC1), intuitively suggest that the level of satisfaction with the communication process between employee and supervisor plays an important part in at least maintaining, if not actually causing, the subjective experience of Frustration, Exhaustion and Defeat. Further more controlled and operationally defined longitudinal study would of course be required to establish the validity of these propositions. Alternative explanations for the relationship between satisfaction

with task related communication and Frustration, Exhaustion and Defeat
suggest that either those experiencing these feelings become
dissatisfied with task related communication, or that dissatisfaction
with task related communication, and the experience of Frustration,
Exhaustion and Defeat reflect the existence of a third variable, itself
correlated with the first subscale of the M.J.B.I. and task related
communication. The former of these explanations remains an unexplored
possibility in the present study. Results of a multiple regression
analysis and the correlations reported in Table 12, while suggesting a
degree of common method variance, do not strongly indicate the
existence of a sufficiently powerful third variable capable of
explaining the relationship between each of the first two subscales of
the M.J.B.I. and satisfaction with task related communication.

Among males, opportunity for Personal Growth and Career
Development (TRNGFAC1) contributed significantly to the regression
equation predicting Frustration, Exhaustion and Defeat. For females
this variable narrowly failed to achieve statistical significance.
The most likely explanation for this sex difference is the difference
in occupational status between the sexes. Many females in the
organisation, in particular those with higher levels of education, are
significantly less satisfied with the training they have received and
the opportunity for further career development (Morris, Note 3). Most
females in the organisation are employed in occupations with limited
career paths. It seems likely that the relatively small numbers of
female employees, compared to males, interested in career development
account for the failure of this variable to achieve statistical

significance in the regression equation. (49% of females in the organisation reported career progress to be very important to them compared with 58% males. Morris, Note 3).

Salary level among males added significantly to the regression equation; those on higher salaries being more likely to experience Frustration, Exhaustion and Defeat. Among females, salary level failed marginally to contribute significantly to the regression equation. This may have resulted from the relatively homogeneous level of earnings among females.

Significant predictors of the Resource Inadequacy subscale of the M.J.B.I. for both sexes included salary level and satisfaction with adequacy of task related communication (CONFAC1). These predictive correlates of the Resource Inadequacy subscale were somewhat stronger and appeared in the reverse order for males compared to females. This result suggests that while the more highly paid employees of both sexes are most likely to experience the feelings of role overload associated with Resource Inadequacy, those on the highest salaries, including the predominantly male management and professional group, are particularly likely to experience the role overload associated with Resource Inadequacy in their work. The reverse order in which these predictors appear in the regression equation for females suggests that women in a broader range of the more senior positions held by them perceive role overload as being more strongly associated with inadequacy of task related communication processes.

Age was a significant predictor of Lowered Self Efficacy, the third subscale of the M.J.B.I., among both sexes. Younger employees, particularly younger females, were more likely to report the lack of confidence at work associated with this subscale of the M.J.B.I.

Salaried status also added significantly to the regression equation for males. This result tentatively suggests that young males in occupations characterised by higher levels of task ambiguity experience lower self efficacy at work. To some extent this conjecture is supported by the marginal failure of the variable opportunity for Personal Growth and Career Development (TRNGFAC1), to achieve significance in the regression equation for males. Items with the heaviest loadings on this predictive variable are concerned with opportunity for training in the organisation. Young males in non-professional salaried occupations are least likely to obtain such training and thus may experience lower levels of self efficacy at work.

Marital status contributed significantly to the regression equation for this subscale of the M.J.B.I. among women. For males it failed marginally to contribute significantly. Young single females are most likely to report low self efficacy at work. Reasons for this are conjectural, particularly since young females are somewhat more satisfied as a group with opportunities for Personal Growth and Career Development than young males. Etzion (1984) has argued that sex differences in socialization processes affect women's expectations of work and their experience of life strain. It may be that younger single women report lower self efficacy at work because they have been subtly conditioned by their socialization to believe that these are appropriate feelings for a young single woman.

Occupational Differences in Subscale Scores on the M.J.B.I.

Scores on the first two subscales of the M.J.B.I. varied significantly for both sexes between occupational groups in the present sample. The pattern of variation on the first subscale of the inventory, Frustration, Exhaustion and Defeat, was very similar for each sex. In general, those occupations characterized by higher levels of decision making discretion scored most highly on this subscale. Each of the occupations in the lower scoring group could be described as being comprised predominantly of more highly structured tasks.

In a multiple regression analysis the relationship between the principal subscale of the M.J.B.I. in the R.C.A., Frustration, Exhaustion and Defeat, and potential work role ambiguity is demonstrated by the principal significant predictor of high scores on this subscale. Employees of both sexes in the R.C.A. reporting higher levels of Frustration, Exhaustion and Defeat are thus also among the most likely to be dissatisfied with the adequacy of a wide range of key factors affecting the way in which they perceive themselves to be managed. Other significant predictors of high scores on this subscale among males suggest that a proportion of the most influential decision makers in the organisation, and many of their potential successors, not only experience burnout but are dissatisfied with their jobs and their future prospects. Salary level is also a significant predictor of Frustration, Exhaustion and Defeat : males on higher salaries being among the most likely to report this component of burnout. The variability of scores on this subscale of burnout both between sexes and occupational types, in particular the difference between male and female non engineering professionals, make it clear that sex differences in burnout, for example that reported by Maslach and Jackson (1981), may well depend on occupational characteristics of the study sample. Higher levels of the burnout component Frustration, Exhaustion and Defeat in the present sample of public sector corporate employees are significantly related to the perceived ineffectiveness of communication between employees and management. Employees of both sexes engaged in the type of work characterised by task ambiguity are more likely to experience feelings of Frustration, Exhaustion and Defeat. Results of a multiple regression analysis suggest that much of the strain associated with work in the K.C.A. arises from task role ambiguity and the perceived incapacity of supervision to provide adequate solutions to the inevitably complex communication problems of a large organisation in conditions of change.

Significant occupational differences in scores on the Resource Inadequacy Subscale of the M.J.B.I. among males follow a similar pattern to that observed for Frustration, Exhaustion and Defeat. The range of scores among different occupational groups on this subscale is narrower than for Frustration, Exhaustion and Defeat. Management and supervision, the group with highest average scores on the first subscale, score close to the average on Resource Inadequacy. When considered in conjunction with the statistically significant predictors of high scores on this subscale among males this result suggests that, among the large group of male engineers and other professionals with higher than average scores, the most senior and highly paid employees experienced more intense feelings of role overload than their supervisors.

In the stage model of burnout proposed by Golembiewski et al. (1983), Emotional Exhaustion is the final stage of burnout. It follows from this that Resource Inadequacy precedes Frustration, Exhaustion and Defeat in the development of burnout. It thus might be reasonably expected that male engineers, the highest scoring group on the Resource Inadequacy subscale of the M.J.B.I. would have among the highest scores on Frustration, Exhaustion and Defeat. This was not found to be the case suggesting that such a stage model of burnout requires further development to take into account the varying responses of different occupational groups to organisational demands.

Multiple regression analysis revealed age to be a significant predictor of Resource Inadequacy among females in addition to Adequacy of Task Related Communication CONFAC1; and salary. Younger females, expressing dissatisfaction with task related communication and earning above average salaries were most likely to experience this component of burnout. Several of the female occupational groups scoring above average on this subscale were among those with high scores on the Lowered Self Efficacy subscale. This result provides some support among females for the model of burnout proposed by Meier (1983) which postulates that expectations for low self efficacy at work lead to overgeneralisation errors and thus burnout.

The significant variation in scores on each of the first two subscales of the M.J.B.I. among different occupational groups, for both sexes, in the absence of such significant differences in scores on the Lowered Self Efficacy subscale provides support for the arguments of Pines, Aronson and Kafry (1981) and Maslach and Jackson (1981) that the stress of the job is the principal cause of burnout.

Scores among different occupational groups on the third subscale of the M.J.B.I., Lowered Self Efficacy, were surprisingly uniform in comparison with the first two subscales and not significantly different statistically. With the exception of management and supervision the trend was for lower expectations of self efficacy among males with occupations characterised by less formal task structure and more decision making discretion. This observation is based on the writers observations of the work performed by each of the occupational groups in the R.C.A. Though not statistically significant the trend is quite clearly apparent in Table 11. At the extremes of the range it is esily recognized that a non engineering professional male, say a personnel officer or a property valuation officer, holds a position with greater decision discretion than say a clerical officer or a storeman. The management and supervision group seem to be an anomolous exception. Managers and supervisors have among the highest self efficacy in their work in spite of the greater discretion they are called upon to exercise. In many respects the essence of the managers role is the resolution of ambiguity in the work setting. The manager is after all charged with responsibility for assisting those who report to him in overcoming their own task ambiguity. Perhaps it is not surprising therefore that managers and supervisors score higher than any other occupational group on the Frustration, Exhaustion and Defeat subscale of the M.J.B.I. It is of course possible that the management group in particular are reluctant to reveal in a survey questionnaire what they perceive as a deficiency in their capacity to cope with the demands of their jobs. When the average scores of the management group on the first two subscales of the inventory are compared with other groups in the organisation it seems likely that managers are either particularly stoical concerning their expectations of self efficacy at work or faking good.

Age and salary status were significant predictors of Lowered Self Efficacy among males in a multiple regression analysis. Younger men employed on salaried as distinct from wages contracts were consistently more likely to have high scores on this subscale of the M.J.B.I.

Score on the independent variable scale Opportunity for Personal Growth and Career Development TRNGFAC1 narrowly failed to achieve statistical significance as a predictor of Lowered Self Efficacy. This result is confirmed by the higher proportion of males employed in occupations with lower expectations of self efficacy who judged their present level of training to be inadequate to perform their present job (E.E.O. Survey Question 35, Morris, Note 3).

The pattern of scores among female occupational groups on the Lowered Self Efficacy subscale differs from that outlined for males and suggests no clear cut interpretation. With the exception of female engineers, a group with the highest level of self efficacy among women, and also the group most satisfied with the training they have received, the data presented in Table 11 suggests that females pursuing traditionally male occupations e.g. Scientists, Drafting Officers and non engineering professionals, score higher on this scale than those in traditionally female occupations. The R.C.A. has an historically enviable record of superior training for young engineers; a record which is reflected in the satisfaction expressed by female engineers. While nothing more than conjecture, the lower level of self efficacy expressed by other professional females may be related to their comparative dissatisfaction with the training and development support they have received in the R.C.A.

Multiple regression analysis revealed age and to a lesser extent marital status to be significant predictors of Lowered Self Efficacy among females; younger and single women being more likely to score high on this subscale. Women in the traditionally male occupations are for historical reasons, more likely to be both young and single. Although score on the Lowered Self Efficacy scale narrowly failed to significantly predict scores on the other two subscales of burnout among women in the R.C.A. significant correlations were found between this subscale and the other two subscales of burnout. It can be seen from Tables 9, 10 and 11 that M.J.B.I. scores are generally higher among women in traditionally male occupations.

Ford et al. (1983) concluded on the basis of their results that burnout as measured by the J.B.I. is independent of episodic or chronic job stress. Recent statistics on claims for compensation arising from work stress in the state of Victoria (Victorian Workcare Report, 1986) indicate that several of the largest classes of claimants, e.g. government and private sector clerical workers of both sexes, typists and office machine operators, are among those with the lowest scores on each of the M.J.B.I. subscales of burnout among similar occupational categories in the R.C.A. Present results taken in conjunction with the Victorian Workcare Statistics thus tend to support the view expressed by Ford et al. (1983) that burnout is substantially independent of chronic job stress.

Berkeley Planning Associates (1977) reported that supervisors of human service workers were less emotionally exhausted than those reporting to them. In the present study the reverse relationship was shown to exist between managers, the highest scoring group on the burnout subscale of Frustration, Exhaustion and Defeat and their subordinates in the R.C.A. On the second subscale of the M.J.B.I., Resource Inadequacy, managers as a group scored lower than other employees in several of the occupational categories.

Ford et al. (1983) observed that little is known about the

incidence of burnout among the occupational groups employed in corporate settings. Corporate sector employees they speculated, are more likely than human service workers to attribute work pressures to a lack of available resources in the organisation. Such attributions in the present sample might explain why those occupations characterized by role ambiguity as measured by question 48 on the E.E.O. survey (Morris, Note 3) which asked "how clear are your work goals" scored higher than management on the Resource Inadequacy subscale of the M.J.B.I. The management group may have the highest scores on the subscale of Frustration, Exhaustion and Defeat as a result of strain arising from the necessity to manage others in conditions of Resource Inadequacy.

As was the case in the present study Ford et al. (1983) found a significant relationship between the Resource Inadequacy subscale and role conflict among corporate sector employees. Higher scores on this subscale among the more senior professionals in the R.C.A. possibly reflect the roles many have as "acting supervisors". This role may involve increased levels of conflicting demands from their own supervisors and those for whom they provide a supervisory role. Such conflicting demands are likely to create precisely the reinforcement conditions described by Pines, Aronson and Kafry (1981) as being characterized by "giving more than is reciprocated".

It is clear from the significant occupational differences in the first two subscales of the M.J.B.I. that those employees with jobs characterised by greater decision making discretion are more at risk for burnout than those with jobs in which tasks are relatively highly structured. The degree of task structure is inferred from the response to question 48 on the E.E.O. survey questionnaire (Morris, Note 3). It seems likely that the current climate of change in the organisation would make its greatest demands on those with the least well defined roles. Key variables in determining the effectiveness of any supervisor subordinate relationship include the quality of interpersonal communication, goal clarity, priority setting and feedback on performance. Those employees in occupations with highest average burnout scores are probably more critically dependent on the quality of supervision they receive to perform their jobs. The incidence of burnout in different occupational groups, and the significant predictors of the subscales comprising it identified in a multiple regression analysis, jointly provide strong evidence in support of burnout in the R.C.A. being predominantly a manifestation of communication dysfunction in the organisation.

The Incidence of Role Overload in Different Work Locations

The incidence of significantly higher scores among males on the Resource Inadequacy subscale of the M.J.B.I., in the absence of similarly elevated scores on the other subscales at those locations characterised by greatest change, lends support to the view that burnout cannot be conceptualised as a unitary phenomenon. Change places a variety of additional demands on those who must work under such conditions; not the least of these are those placed upon the communication processes. Ineffectual communication processed have

been cited by several authors in the burnout literature to be involved
in the development of burnout. Pines, Aronson and Kafry (1981)
argued that perceptions of such defective communication lead to
frustration and eventually burnout. Berkeley Planning Associates
(1977) found adequacy of communication processes to be a significant
predictor of burnout and Sharit and Salvendy (1982) concluded that
increasing uncertainty arising from poorly planned change and
inadequately defined work goals constituted the final common pathway
of dysfunctional stress.

In a multiple regression analysis of the present data score on
the dependent variable scale, Adequacy of Task Related Communication
CONFAC1, predicted a significant proportion of variance on the
Resource Inadequacy subscale of the M.J.B.I. for both sexes. For the
following reasons it seems reasonable to conjecture that the role
overload associated with Resource Inadequacy is more likely to precede
Frustration, Exhaustion and Defeat as a stage in the development of
burnout than the reverse as suggested by Stout and Williams (1983).
It could reasonably be expected that if significant differences were
observed in scores on any of the subscales of the M.J.B.I. between
work locations such differences would first be observed in those
components of burnout developing earliest in the process. If
Frustration, Exhaustion and Defeat preceded Resource Inadequacy in the
developmental process of burnout such differences could perhaps have
been observed on this subscale. They were not however and this
suggests that the model of progressive burnout proposed by
Golembiewski, Munzenrider and Carter (1983), in which Emotional

Exhaustion follows Depersonalisation and Diminished Personal Accomplishment, is more likely to describe the temporal sequence of burnout than that suggested by Stout and Williams (1983)

Males in the R.C.A. are significantly more likely to score high on the Resource Inadequacy scale of the M.J.B.I. than females. It is possible that work locations at which males score significantly higher on the Resource Inadequacy subscale may exhibit this characteristic partly as a function of the mix of occupational categories employed in those locations. Among male employees engineers and survey officers are among those scoring highest on the Resource Inadequacy subscale. Both of these groups tend to be overrepresented on new construction work and this may have contributed to a significant result which is more economically explained by occupational differences alone.

No statistically significant variation was found in the subscale scores of any occupational category. As the sample was both stratified and randomly selected it seems likely that the significant result owes its existence, at least in part, to some distinctive features of the work situation in those locations with significantly higher scores on the Resource Inadequacy subscale. It is suggested that one of these distinctive features is an overloading of the task related communication network. Such conditions were reported as the primary stressor in conditions of uncertainty by Drabek and Haas (1969).

In the model of burnout proposed by Meier (1983) expectations of self efficacy are hypothesised to be a determinant of the burnout process. No significant differences were apparent between locations in scores on either of the other subscales of the M.J.B.I., Frustration, Exhaustion and Defeat or Lowered Self Efficacy . Thus it appears from the present result tht feelings of lowered self efficacy are are not a prerequisite for the onset of burnout : at least as far as the hypothesized component of Resource Inadequacy is concerned.

The Experience of Burnout Among Different Demographic Subgroups

Sex Differences in Burnout

Males in the present sample are significantly more likely than females to report higher scores on the second subscale of the M.J.B.I.. Resource Inadequacy describes feelings of strain arising principally from the belief that personal resources, particularly time, are inadequate to cope with demands of both work and private life. Males in the organisation, apart from being older and longer serving on average than females, perform a substantially different range of work. Males who reported higher scores on the subscale of Resource Inadequacy are employed in occupations among which there is the lowest female participation rate. It is thus the marked gender difference in occupational type which is most likely to account for the significantly higher scores among males on the second subscale of the M.J.B.I.

Maslach and Jackson (1981), having reported female human service
workers to be significantly more burned out than males, cautioned that
the sex differences may be confounded with occupational type. Results
reported here for each of the subscales of M.J.B.I. suggest that type
of occupation is a consistently more powerful determinant of the
burnout experience at work than gender. The existing literature on
stress and burnout e.g Etzion (1984) and Osipow Doty and Spokane
(1985), has been equivocal concerning sex differences in work related
burnout. Present results suggest that inconsistency of reported sex
differences in work related burnout may well be explained by occupational
differences in the various samples selected for study.

The sex differences on the first subscale of the M.J.B.I.,
Frustration, Exhaustion and Defeat, for the sample as a whole was not
statistically significant. As with Resource Inadequacy there were
significant differences in scores on the subscale between occupational
groups for both sexes. It follows from this that a significant sex
difference could have emerged for Frustration, Exhaustion and Defeat
depending on the occupational characteristic of the sample. If for
example the sample used in the present study had included a greater
proportion of female supervisors, technical and non technical
professionals, administrative officers and secretaries, it seems very
likely that a significant sex difference would have been reported :
females in such a sample having the potential for higher scores than
males on the subscale Frustration, Exhaustion, and Defeat. The
results reported here suggest that burnout research among corporate
sector employees, depending on subjects responses to items included in

an inventory, should ensure adequate sampling to control for sex and occupational differences in burnout.

Age Differences

Human service workers of both sexes have been consistently reported to experience significantly higher levels of burnout early in their careers. Male employees of the R.C.A. in the age range 30 to 49 were significantly more likely than younger or older men to be high scorers on the Resource Inadequacy subscale of the M.J.B.I. This result suggests that males employed in the present public sector organisation, as was reported for male teachers by Metz (1979), experience at least some forms of stressful work conditions more intensely at critical stages in their careers. Since the significant age difference was not confounded with occupational type it seems likely that the demands of work in the present public sector corporate organisation differ from those existing in human service work. Explanations must of course remain speculative conjuecture but perhaps the most likely concerns the inevitable mid career crisis postulated by Cardinell (1981) who suggested that certain career development stages are ripe for burnout because commitment to work ideals is larger than the sense of satisfaction from work at these times. The notion of such a mid career "crisis" is explicable in the competitive career structure in corporate sector organisations. Males in the age range 30 to 49 are faced with a greater degree of competitive performance pressure to obtain promotion than younger or older men. Many males with aspirations for promotion are necessarily disappointed and must come to terms with this. It may be that by the age of 50 males are able to make a realistic assessment of their own potential for further career development, come to terms with this, and experience lower levels of stress and strain as reported by Osipow, Doty and Spokane (1985). It is feasible that the results reported by Metz (1979) are explained by similar competitive pressure for promotion among male teachers in this age range.

Young employees of both sexes in the R.C.A. were significantly more likely to report high scores on the Lowered Self Efficacy subscale of the M.J.B.I. This result is consistent with that reported by Maslach and Jackson (1981) who found that young human service workers were significantly more likely to express feelings of low personal accomplishment than older members of this group. According to the stage model of burnout proposed by Golembiewski et al. (1983) a sense of diminished personal accomplishment precedes emotional exhaustion in the development of burnout. The model thus suggests that organisations in which young employees experience feelings of lowered self efficacy for prolonged periods will be prone to higher levels of burnout. Osipow, Doty and Spokane (1985) asserted that many older workers learn to use coping strategies which enhance their ability to experience reduced strain given equal amounts of stress. Some younger employees, unable or unwilling to adopt such coping strategies, leave the organisation or field work in order to resolve unacceptable levels of stress. Scores on the Lowered Self Efficacy subscale of the M.J.B.I. failed in a multiple regression analysis to account for a statistically significant proportion of variance in scores on either of the subscales of the M.J.B.I. This result could be expected if younger employees reporting lower expectations of self efficacy leave the organisation before burning out thus moderating the relationship between these variables in the organisation. Low levels of labour turnover in the R.C.A. suggest this is unlikely to be the case.

Ford et al. (1983) concluded that human service workers process information about stressful work conditions differently from corporate sector employees. They speculated that whereas a human service worker might attribute intense time pressures to a lack of personal autonomy, employees in corporate settings may attribute similiar pressures to insufficient organisational resources. The significantly lower expectations of self efficacy expressed among younger employees in the R.C.A. may thus at a later stage in career development, as suggested by the present results, be attributed to Resource Inadequacy in the organisation.

Pines, Aronson and Kafry (1981) asserted that burnout was more likely to occur among younger employees. From this assertion it could have been predicted that, like the younger human service workers reported by Berkeley Planning Associates (1977) and Maslach and Jackson (1981), younger employees in the R.C.A., a large public sector bureaucracy, would be significantly more likely to experience burnout. The observation that no such age differences were apparent for either sex on the first two subscales of the M.J.B.I., Frustration,

Exhaustion and Defeat and Resource Inadequacy lends support to the conclusion of Ford et al. (1983) that corporate sector employees process information about stressful work conditions to some extent differently than human service workers. The existence of such differences should not obscure similarities in the way younger persons, regardless of gender, experience the type of work conditions leading to burnout. The observation that younger employees of both sexes in the R.C.A. reported significantly lower levels of self efficacy at work is consistent with the results of Maslach and Jackson (1981) who reported younger employees in human service work to have significantly lower self reported expectations of personal accomplishment.

It is suggested that younger employees in public sector corporate organisations, such as the R.C.A., are not vulnerable to burnout in the same way as their age mates providing human service care for at least two reasons. First, the type of problem solving activity characteristic of work in such organisations does not make the same level of emotional demand on young employees as that experienced by a young human service worker who must, as Berkeley Planning Associates (1977) asserted, use himself or herself as the technology in meeting the needs of clients. Second, young corporate sector employees, whatever their discipline or level of education, are rarely if ever given the impression that they will take a significant degree of individual responsibility for the outcome of their decisions at work early in their careers. Thus the expectations they hold concerning work outcomes may be more modest than those held by human service workers.

Burnout and Marital Status

Single and divorced subjects of both sexes in the present study scored higher than those who were married on the first subscale of the M.J.B.I., Frustration, Exhaustion and Defeat. Divorced subjects had the highest scores on this subscale. These results, though not statistically significant, are worthy of mention as they are as would have been predicted from the results of Maslach and Jackson (1981). Maslach and Jackson (1981) reported significantly higher scores among single and divorced human service workers on the Emotional Exhaustion subscale of the M.B.I. Failure of the present results relating to the first subscale of the M.J.B.I. to achieve statistical significance may be due to the much smaller number of single and divorced subjects in the sample.

The statistical significance of lower scores among married females on the third subscale of the M.J.B.I., Lowered Self Efficacy, suggests at face value that married women have higher expectations of self efficacy at work than those who are single or divorced. Since older females to a greater extent than older men, are significantly less likely to score high on Lowered Self Efficacy, it seems quite possible that this result primarily reflects differences in age rather than marital status.

Relationship between Role Overload and Level of Education

The significant relationship among males between level of education and score on the M.J.B.I. subscale of Resource Inadequacy indicated that more highly educated males experienced greater levels of strain associated with role overload in their jobs. The same trend was apparent for females but narrowly failed to achieve statistical significance. Occupational differences between the sexes are most likely to explain this result. Males in the sample were educationally a more heterogeneous group than females. Engineers for example, the highest scoring occupational group on the Resource Inadequacy subscale, are all tertiary qualified and male engineers outnumber females by more than 14 to 1. It is not unlikely that a similiar level of educational heterogeneity among females would have resulted in a statistically significant differences in scores on the Resource Inadequacy subscale of the M.J.B.I.

Maslach and Jackson (1981) reported more highly educated human service workers to be significantly more emotionally exhausted. The absence of a significant relationship between level of education and score on the first subscale of the M.J.B.I., Frustration, Exhaustion and Defeat, provides some further evidence of occupational differences in the experience of burnout. Occupations with the highest scores on the first subscale, Frustration, Exhaustion and Defeat, were those requiring the highest level of interpersonal functioning e.g. Management and Supervision, Non Engineering Professionals and Secretaries. In a sense these occupations provide the closest parallel with human service workers. Occupational heterogeneity in

the present sample, particularly among males, may have obscured to
some extent the relationship between M.J.B.I. scale scores and
education level. Some further evidence for this proposition is
provided by the trend among the more highly educated females toward
higher scores on the subscale. This trend, while not statistically
significant was notably stronger among females than males.

As with the relationship between level of education and the
Personal Accomplishment scale of burnout reported by Maslach and
Jackson (1981), no consistent trend was found between the Lowered Self
Efficacy subscale and education levels. Expectations of job related
self efficacy thus appear to be independent of education level in the
present study organisation.

Relationship between Role Overload and Salary Level

A consistent relationship exists, for both sexes in the R.C.A.,
between salary level and scores on the M.J.B.I. subscale Resource
Inadequacy : higher salaries being in general associated with greater
self reported strain. This result suggests that those in positions of
greater responsibility experience more role overload. In fact the
most highly paid males, management and supervision, report only
slightly above average scores on this subscale of burnout. Feelings
reflecting Resource Inadequacy arising from role overload are
experienced most intensely by professional employees of both sexes.
Among females, secretaries also reported higher scores on this
subscale; secretaries in the R.C.A. are expected to fulfil many of the

roles of personal assistant and thus must exercise decision
making discretion.

In general, employees earning lower salaries occupy
positions characterised by greater task structure. The task
content of these occupational groups also makes less acute demands on
employees for effective interpersonal functioning in performance of
the work. It is suggested that the significant relationship between
salary and score on the Resource Inadequacy subscale is best explained
by the level of uncertainty which must be tolerated by those in the
more highly paid, but less well structured occupations. It would be
consistent with this explanation that those receiving the highest
salaries, management and supervision, score less highly on this
subscale because they have greater decision making discretion and thus
more control over work outcomes.

Relationship Between Subscales of the M.J.B.I. and Work Measures
Comparable with those Reported by Ford, Murphy and Edwards (1983)

The significant negative correlations reported in Table 8, for
males and females between the first subscale of the M.J.B.I.,
Frustration, Exhaustion and Defeat and all work outcome measures
comparable to those reported by Ford et al. (1983) provide support for
their results. They concluded that, while human service workers may
process information about stressful work conditions differently from
corporate sector employees, those experiencing burnout in each group
are likely to be dissatisfied with similar facets of the job

situation.

Relationship between the Subscales of the M.J.B.I. and Satisfaction with Type of Work

The significant negative correlation, among males between satisfaction with type of work performed and the Resource Inadequacy subscale was not found among corporate sector employees in the results reported by Ford et al. (1983). The present result suggests at least the two following possible explanations. First, that those who obtain less than adequate satisfaction from the type of work they do are more vulnerable to strain from role overload: second, that those who experience feelings of Resource Inadequacy at work become less satisfied with the type of work they do. Since overall satisfaction in present position (CONFAC2) was not a significant predictor of Resource Inadequacy in the multiple regression analysis reported here, whereas adequacy of task related communication (CONFAC1) predicted a significant proportion of total variance in Resource Inadequacy the second possible explanation seems more likely. This explanation is consistent both with the results of Berkeley Planning Associates (1977), who found poor communication to be a significant predictor of burnout among human service workers, and the model of burnout proposed by Meier (1983). In Meier's model expectations of self efficacy are determined in part by repeated learning experiences on the job. If males repeatedly experience low expectations of positive reinforcement on the job as a result of Resource Inadequacy it follows from Meier's model that self efficacy expectations will diminish leading to dissatisfaction with the type of work performed. This explanation is of course substantially conjectural since the correlation in question, although statistically significant, is very small. The result reported here does suggest that further development and testing of the parsimonious cognitive model of burnout proposed by Meier (1983) may help to explain at least some of the crucial determinants of individual differences in burnout.

Among females the correlation between Resource Inadequacy and satisfaction with type of work performed was very small. This result suggests either that the feelings associated with Resource Inadequacy at work are independent of satisfaction with the type of work peformed by women or it might, which seems less likely, suggest indifference on the part of women to the type of work they do. Since adequacy of task related communication (CONFAC1) is a significant predictor of Resource Inadequacy among females, and women with high scores on the subscale of Resource Inadequacy are less satisfied with goal clarity and feedback on performance than men, it seems more likely that this aspect of burnout affects women regardless of how satisfied they are with the type of work they perform.

Lowered Self Efficacy was negatively correlated with satisfaction with the type of work for both sexes. This correlation achieved statistical significance for males but not for females. Salary earning status accounted for a statistically significant proportion of variance in scores on the Lowered Self Efficacy subscale of the M.J.B.I. among males in a multiple regression analysis but not among the proportionally larger group of salaried females. The regression equation suggests that the relationship between expectations of low self efficacy at work and satisfaction with type of work performed is stronger among the salaried males than those engaged on wages contracts. Wage-earning males perform the type of work usually described as artisan or unskilled labour. The schedule on which salaried males might experience a variety of negative reinforcement in the work situation would undoubtedly have greater potential to induce the expectations of lowered self efficacy postulated by Meier (1983). The hypothesized process of behaviourally conditioned lowered expectations of self efficacy given by Meier (1983) is consistent with the present results. The groups of male employees with lowest expectations of self efficacy at work are in general those who occupations involve the highest potential for ambiguity and thus negative reinforcement and work role dissatisfaction.

Relationship between the Subscales of the M.J.B.I. and Satisfaction with Supervision

Resource Inadequacy was significantly negatively correlated among males with all four measures of satisfaction with supervision. Among females three of the four items reflecting satisfaction with supervision were significantly negatively correlated with Resource Inadequacy. The level of satisfaction among females with the working relationship shared by them with their supervisors, the fourth item, failed to reach statistical significance, the correlation for this item being notably smaller than for the other three. This result suggests the following possible explanations. First, that females experiencing feelings of strain arising from role overload see this as being largely independent of their relationship with their supervisor, i.e. the supervisor is not the cause of the feelings associated with Resource Inadequacy. Second, that while females experiencing role overload associated with Resource Inadequacy are dissatisfied with some aspects of the supervision they receive, they are prepared to maintain largely satisfactory relationships despite this, i.e. they are more tolerant of poor supervision.

Since adequacy of task related communication (CONFAC1) was a significant predictor of Resource Inadequacy among females in the second explanation seems more likely. Again this reasoning is conjectural to a large extent but is is consistent with the observation that females are significantly less likely than men to report role overload as measured by the Resource Inadequacy subscale of the M.J.B.I. If females are in fact more tolerant of less than adequate supervision it could be expected that they would report higher levels of self efficacy at work. Since they did not this provides some further evidence that expectations of self efficacy at work are independent of the feelings of role overload reflected in scores on the Resource Inadequacy subscale of the M.J.B.I. among females.

Females most likely to have high scores on the Lowered Self Efficacy subscale are those who are both young and single. Each of these variables contributes significantly to prediction of score on this subscale of the M.J.B.I. among females. The positive correlations among females between Lowered Self Efficacy and three of the four items relating to satisfaction with supervision suggest that the less confident females, likely to be young and single, may at the earliest stages of their working life have lower expectations of the supervision they receive from predominantly male supervisors.

Relationship between the Subscales of the M.J.B.I. and Satisfaction with Pay

The significant negative correlation for each sex between the Resource Inadequacy subscale of the M.J.B.I. and satisfaction with pay was stronger than that reported by Ford et al. (1983). Among corporate sector employees in the Ford et al. (1983) study this correlation failed to achieve statistical significance. Among human service workers in the same study satisfaction with pay was significantly negatively correlated with three of the five subscales of burnout reported for human service workers including the Supportless Organisation subscale. This subscale contains two of the items comprising the Resource Inadequacy subscale of the M.J.B.I..

One possible explanation of the difference in results suggested by the relatively short average job tenure of subjects in the Ford et al. (1983) study, may be the comparative heterogeneity in length of job tenure in the present sample. Employees with longer tenure may be closer to the limits of their capacity for career development and thus more likely to express dissatisfaction with pay. This explanation while conjectural is consistent with level of salary being significantly predictive of the Resource Inadequacy subscale of the

M.J.B.I. among males and females in the R.C.A.; higher salaries being predictive of greater self reported strain from role overload.

Among females a significant positive correlation between Lowered Self Efficacy and satisfaction with pay suggested that women with lower levels of self confidence at work are more likely to be satisfied with their remuneration. This result is consistent with the notion that women with lower levels of self confidence are more tolerant of what they perceive as less than adequate supervision in the organisation.

Relationship between the Subscales of the M.J.B.I. and Satisfaction with Future Prospects

Significant negative correlations for both sexes between each of the subscales of the M.J.B.I. and satisfaction with future prospects suggest that negative expectations concerning career development play a more prominent role in burnout among the present public sector corporate subjects than among either the human service workers or private sector corporate subjects in the Ford et al. study. Satisfaction with promotion prospects among the private sector corporate employees in the Ford et al. (1983) study was significantly negatively correlated with Emotional Exhaustion and Defeat but not with Resource Inadequacy. The present sample was drawn from a mature and stable bureaucracy in which negative expectations for further promotion may well be realistically justifiable for many employees, particularly the young, and those with long service. Negative expectations for future career development in the present sample may thus intensify the feelings of role overload characteristic of Resource Inadequacy. It seems likely that such negative expectations would have been less pronounced among the private corporate sector employees reported by Ford et al. (1983) since they had very much shorter job tenure.

The significant negative correlation reported here between scores on the Lowered Self Efficacy subscale of the M.J.B.I. and satisfaction with future prospects is not surprising since present expectations of self efficacy and those associated with future personal development must surely be closely related.

Relationship between the Subscales of the M.J.B.I. and Satisfaction with Goal Clarity of Feedback on Performance

The significant negative correlation for each sex between the first two subscales of the M.J.B.I. and satisfaction with goal clarity is supportive of the conclusion made by Ford et al. (1983) that structuring of activities by supervisors is stress reducing. The relationship reported by Ford et al. (1983) between the Resource Inadequacy subscale and measures of role ambiguity and informational support at work among private sector corporate employees failed to reach statistical significance. The significance of the negative relationship between Resource Inadequacy and goal clarity in the present study of public sector employees suggests at least the following possibilities. First, that employees of the R.C.A. experience the feelings of role overload associated with Resource

Inadequacy as a result of inadequately defined goals. Second, that

dissatisfaction with goal clarity arises from role overload as part of

a more general dissatisfaction with stressful work conditions. Third,

and perhaps more likely than either of these explanations in view of

the significant negative relationship between the first two subscales

of burnout and satisfaction with the amount of work expected by

supervision, is that each of the first two conditions interact to

sustain the experience the burnout. Failure of the relationship

between Resource Inadequacy and role ambiguity to reach statistical

significance in the Ford et al. (1983) study is suprising since the

experience of conflicting demands at work comprises one component of

their Resource Inadequacy subscale. A conjectural though feasible

explanation of the results reported by Ford et al. (1983) is suggested

by the more tangible work output criteria characteristic of private

sector corporations. The Ford et al. (1983) result was consistent

with the corporate sector employees in their sample experiencing less

role ambiguity and more adequate informational support from

supervision as a result of their having more clearly defined goals

than the present sample of public service employees.

Similar negative relationships to those found between the first

two subscales of the M.J.B.I. and satisfaction with goal clarity were

found between these subscales and satisfaction with feedback on

performance. The correlation between the subscale scores and

satisfaction with feedback on performance was higher than that between

each of them and satisfaction with goal clarity. This result provides

support for the tentative conclusion of Snyder and Morris (1984) that

the quality of performance feedback is of greater importance for

individual feelings of self efficacy at work than the overall quality
of the supervisors communication. The result is also consistent with
that of Maslacn and Jackson (1981) who found a significant negative
correlation between scores on the knowledge of results scale of the
Job Diagnostic Survey and burnout. They concluded that human service
workers scoring nigh on each of the subscales of the M.J.B.I. did not
know now effectively tney were performing their jobs. In eacn case
the results support the speculative conclusion of Ford et al. (1983)
that contrary to their original expectations, efforts by supervisors
to provide task structure is stress reducing by limiting tne ambiguity
associatea with the job. Correlations between the Lowereu Self
Efficacy subscale of the M.J.B.I. and satisfaction witn goal clarity
and feedback on pertormance were non existent or very low for ootn
sexes. This result suggests that expectations of selt efficacy at
work are independent ot each of these measures of work satisfaction.

Ford et al. (1983) cited the negative relationsnip in tneir
stuay between burnout and symptoms of poor nealtn, aosence arising
from illness and episodic job stress as eviaence tnat the burnout
construct is independent of tne strain associateu witn tnese
variables. They concluded that while numan service workers and
corporate sector employees may process information aoout stressful job
conditions differently, eacn group was aissatisfied witn a broadly
similiar range of interpersonal facets of tneir job situation.
Present results proviae general support for tne validity of their
conclusions among employees of a large public sector bureaucracy.

Relationship Between Burnout and Disability

The only statistically significant relationship between
disability and the M.J.B.I. was found among males between the first
two subscales and the generic category of "Other disability including
chronic illness/pain". This relationship suggests that at least some
chronic health problems may exacerbate the experience of burnout. No
substantive explanation of this result is possible owing to the
generic nature of the item. Since most other forms of occupationally
relevant disability were dealt with specifically in the E.E.O.
question on disability it seems reasonable to assume that most of the
males reporting moderate or severe "Other disability" were suffering
chronic pain. Ford et al. (1983) rejected the notion that health
problems and chronic job stress are related to burnout among corporate
sector employees. The present result suggests that further
investigation of this relationship is required before burnout may be
viewed as independent of chronic health problems. It is interesting
to note that no significant relationship was found between this or any
other form of disability and the Lowered Self Efficacy subscale of the
M.J.B.I.

Relationship Between the M.J.B.I. and Opportunity for Personal
Growth and Career Development

Research included significant negative correlations between
scores on the Opportunity for Personal Growth and Career Development
(TRNGFAC1) scale derived from factor analysis of E.E.O. survey

questionnaire items and each of the M.J.B.I. subscales. The results
suggest a similiar relationship between these variables among public
sector corporate employees to that reported by Maslach (1976) and
Maslach and Jackson (1981) among human service workers. Maslach and
Jackson (1981) found a significant negative relationship between
burnout and scores on the Job Diagnostic Survey "Growth Satisfaction"
scale (Hackman and Oldham, 1975).

In a multiple regression analysis scores on the scale TRNGFAC1
predicted a significant proportion of variance among males on the
first subscale of burnout : Frustration, Exhaustion and Defeat.
TRNGFAC1 narrowly failed to predict a statistically significant
proportion of variance in the Resource Inadequacy and Lowered Self
Efficacy subscales among males ($p = .08$). The TRNGFAC1 scale also
narrowly failed to predict a significant proportion of variance in the
Resource Inadequacy subscale among females ($p = .06$).

Pines, Aronson and Kafry (1981) asserted that burnout affects
many who earlier in their careers had been among the most committed
and enthusiastic. The disappointment of career development
aspirations appears to play a part in the experience of burnout among
both sexes in the R.C.A. Inclusion of scores on the TRNGFAC1 scale as
a statistically significant or near significant predictor of burnout
suggests that the experience of burnout may be more clearly understood
following further exploration of the role of expectations for personal
development in organisational settings.

Some Implications of the Present Results for Models of Burnout In
Organisations

Although significant correlations were found between self
efficacy expectations at work and each of the first two subscales of
the M.J.B.I. the present results provide only limited support for the
model of burnout proposed by Meier (1983). The correlations were not
large and the Lowered Self Efficacy scale failed to predict a
significant proportion of variance in either of the other subscales.

The causal explanation of burnout in Meier's model suggests
that both expectations for self efficacy at work and those for
satisfactory work outcomes outside the control of the individual are
combined in a causal system with reciprocal effects. Meier
acknowledged that very little theoretical or empirical evidence
exists from which predictions can be made concerning the relative
importance of each of these in the process of burnout.

Several work measures previously identified in the burnout
literature relating to human service workers were found to be more
strongly correlated than the Lowered Self Efficacy subscale of the
M.J.B.I. with each of the other two subscales. In addition, these
correlates were significant components of regression equations for the
two principal subscales of the M.J.B.I. It is tentatively suggested
based on the present results that the relationship between burnout and
work outcome expectations is perhaps stronger than that between
burnout and expectations for self efficacy at work. Adequacy of task

related communication has been shown to be significantly more strongly

related to the experience of Frustration, Exhaustion and Defeat, in

the R.C.A. than have expectations for self efficacy at work. Although

a speculative conjecture at this stage it is possible that the level

of dissatisfaction is itself partly determined by the individual's

expectations of self efficacy at work thus forming a causal system for

burnout of the type with reciprocal effects postulated by Meier

(1983).

Such a causal system could be described thus : when the

individual's capacity for tolerance of work ambiguity, determined in

part by his expectations of self efficacy, reaches a critical point

the individual will show early signs of burnout. This was

hypothesized by Golembiewski et al. (1983) and Pines et al. (1981) to

be a deterioration of the sense of personal accomplishment.

Such a model should not prove too difficult to operationalize

as the next step in development of the model of burnout proposed by

Meier (1983). Results reported here suggest that subject samples for

such developmental work should be carefully matched for occupational

type.

Osipow and Spokane (1983) postulated that given equal amounts

of stress, strain varies as a function of coping capacity. This

model is more general than either of the others considered here;

however, if the predictions of Osipow and Spokane are supported

by empirical evidence it would suggest that any model of burnout

should take account of individual differences in coping.
Assuming that the level of expected self efficacy at work is a
reliable indicator of capacity to cope under stressful conditions
it could be expected that those employees reporting significantly
higher levels of burnout would report lower levels of expected
self efficacy at work. The size of the correlations reported
here suggests that either the level of expected self efficacy at
work is not a reliable estimator of the capacity to cope or that
the model proposed by Osipow and Spokane (1983) requires further
refinement before it can be considered useful in the development
of models of burnout among corporate sector employees.

The significant positive correlations between the Lowered Self
Efficacy subscale of the M.J.B.I. and each of the subscales
hypothesised by Ford et al. (1983) to be components of burnout among
corporate sector employees provides a limited degree of support for the
coping model of Osipow and Spokane (1983). Osipow, Doty and Spokane
(1985) found younger subjects reported experiencing significantly more
strain and lower coping capacity than older subjects. Results of a
multiple regression analysis in the present study revealed age to be a
significant predictor of score on the Lowered Self Efficacy scale :
younger subjects of both sexes being significantly more likely to
report Lowered Self Efficacy. The marginal failure of scores on the
Lowered Self Efficacy subscale of the M.J.B.I. to account for a
significant proportion of variance in either of the two subscales of
burnout as postulated in the model of burnout proposed by Meier (1983)

may thus be due to the different age distributions of scores on the burnout scales compared with the Lowered Self Efficacy scale.

Gertz (1979) conjectured without specifying a theoretical explanation that it is perhaps possible for a whole organisation to reach the point of burnout. For a whole organisation to become progressively burned out it would seem likely that some groups of individuals in the organisation comprising a recognisable subsystem, either of an occupational specialist or geographic nature, would show the earliest signs of the burnout phenomenon before others. Present results have shown that some groups in the R.C.A. report significantly higher levels of burnout than others. Such differences suggest that it is feasible as Gertz (1979) has suggested for at least parts of an organisation, and therefore perhaps whole organisations, to become burned out.

No attempt has been made to the present authors knowledge to formulate a model of the burnout construct in terms of any theory of organisational behaviour. Results reported here suggest that burnout in the R.C.A. reflects potentially important features of a communication deficit in the relationships between individuals and their supervisors. The pheonomenon of burnout in the R.C.A. can thus be conceptualized as a property of the current level of functioning of the organisation system as a whole, rather than as has often been assumed in the literature, the outcome of work related stress and strain among those individuals less able to cope with the demands of particular kinds of work.

Significant predictors of the subscales of burnout reported here in a multiple regression analysis are consistent with the results reported by Berkeley Planning Associates (1977). A stage model of burnout similiar to that proposed by Golembiewski et al. (1983) and including one or more organisation system variables shown to have statistical relevance in the prediction of burnout may prove sufficiently robust to be useful in more experimental designs of burnout research aimed at uncovering causal factors. A stage model of burnout including organisation variables may prove easier to operationalize and test than more theoretically complex models of burnout such as that proposed by Meier (1983). Development of such a stage model of burnout in organisations would of course require analysis of a range of relevant objective organisational outcome variables in addition to data collected in the form of responses to a reliable burnout instrument. Present results suggest that a more adequate theoretical explanation of the burnout phenomenon is likely to depend on consideration of the characteristics of the organisational system in which it occurs. Where statistically significant differences in burnout were found between geographically separate work groups and different occupational categories in the R.C.A. these can at best be only incompletely explained by the models of burnout considered here and require speculative reference to their determinants in the organisation subsystem in which they are manifest.

Some Implications of the Present Results for an Organisational
Response to Burnout

Exploration of the relationship between high levels of burnout
in the R.C.A. and the dysfunctional effects reported in the burnout
literature to be associated with the phenomenon was beyond the scope
of the present study. Meier (1983) pointed out that the choice of an
appropriate intervention to deal with the effects of burnout will
depend on reliable knowledge of what is being targetted for
intervention.

Stress management training programs in a variety of forms
including some, such as those proposed by Pines, Aronson and Kafry
(1981), Veniga and Spradley (1981) claimed to combat burnout, have
become an increasingly common attempt to cope with the symptoms of job
stress. Many stress management programs fail to obtain reliable
knowledge concerning the source of the stress they are supposed to
manage and where evaluation has occurred the results according to
Ganster, Mayes, Sime and Tharp (1982) are equivocal. It is a basic
assumption of many of these programs that stress innoculation of
individuals constitutes useful remedial action. Altering the
reactions of employees to presumed noxious and stressful
organisational, task and role characteristics does not in fact remove
stressors from the employees organisational environment. Such
training can thus be considered ineffectual at best and downright
unethical at worst. Training employees to better tolerate poorly
designed and managed organisations seems a less effective strategy for

all concerned than one which attempts to remove the known causes of dysfunctional stress arising within the organisation.

Present results suggest that the development of improved coping strategies at the individual level, while it may go some way towards ameliorating the effects of burnout in the short term, will be largely ineffective and possibly counterproductive in the longer term. Those in the organisation experiencing both high levels of Frustration, Exhaustion and Defeat and dissatisfaction with task related communication may perceive such attempts to improve their capacity to cope as further evidence of their own personal failure.

Summary of Results and Conclusions

The factor structure of the M.J.B.I. derived from the present sample of public sector corporate employees, although not identical with that reported by Ford et al. (1983) for private sector employees is comprised of substantially similar subscales. Ford et al.'s speculative conclusion that human service workers process information about stressful work conditions differently from corporate sector employees is only tentatively supported by the present results. While the first two subscales of the M.J.B.I. in the R.C.A. closely approximate those reported by Ford et al. (1983) for corporate sector employees the third subscale of the M.J.B.I., Lowered Self Efficacy, suggests that the feelings of diminished personal accomplishment identified by Maslach and Jackson (1981) are a component of burnout in both human service and corporate sector groups.

The Job Burnout Inventory of Ford et al. (1983) has been criticised here for excluding items designed to measure feelings of personal accomplishment. Personal accomplishment emerged as the second factor subscale of burnout following Emotional Exhaustion in the Maslach Burnout Inventory developed by Maslach and Jackson (1981) to assess burnout among human service workers. The proportion of total variance explained by the first two subscales of the M.J.B.I. is neither comparable with that reported by Ford et al. (1983) nor indicative that the scale adequately measures burnout among corporate sector employees. Present results suggest that the M.J.B.I. will be improved by the addition of further items designed to measure more precisely expectations of diminished personal accomplishment and self efficacy at work. It is cautiously conjectured that refinement of the item content of the M.J.B.I. relating to feelings of diminished personal accomplishment and lowered self efficacy may have the result of replacing Resource Inadequacy as the second subscale of burnout among corporate sector employees with a subscale reflecting the experience of diminished personal accomplishment. In the event that such a subscale accounted for a significantly greater proportion of variance than the Resource Inadequacy subscale it will be shown that the experience of burnout among human service and corporate sector employees shares more common features than is suggested by the conclusions of Ford et al. (1983).

It seems likely that the significant sex differences in scores on the second scale of the M.J.B.I. found in the present study and those differences previously reported in the burnout literature, particularly that associated with emotional exhaustion, are confounded with sex differences in occupational status among the samples studied: scores on each of the first two subscales of the M.J.B.I. were found to vary significantly by occupational group for both sexes in the R.C.A..

Scores on the second subscale of the M.J.B.I., Resource Inadequacy, were found to vary significantly among males of different ages in the present sample. Males between 30 and 49 years of age were significantly more likely to score highly on this subscale providing some support for the notion of a mid career "crisis" among males proposed by Cardinell (1981). The absence of a similar significant difference across the life span in the first subscale of the M.J.B.I., Frustration, Exhaustion and Defeat, suggests that this "crisis" is associated with perceptions of role overload at work but not burnout as suggested by Cardinell (1981).

Correlational evidence was found in support of the model of burnout proposed by Meier (1983). Correlations between each of the first two subscales of the M.J.B.I. and expectations of self efficacy at work although statistically significant were small. In a multiple regression analysis scores on the third subscale of the M.J.B.I., Lowered Self Efficacy, failed to account for a statistically significant proportion of variance in either of the first two subscales of the M.J.B.I. in the R.C.A.. The model of burnout proposed by Meier (1983) depends on outcome expectations in addition to those for self efficacy at work. Present results tentatively suggest that outcome expectations may be a more powerful determinant of the burnout experience than those for self efficacy at work. Future research may demonstrate than an understanding of the interaction of outcome expectations and those for self efficacy is necessary before validation of this model of burnout is possible.

Scores on the first two subscales of the M.J.B.I. varied significantly between occupational groups for both sexes. Those occupations subjectively classified as having greater decision discretion and higher levels of task ambiguity being more likely to score high on the subscales associated with burnout among corporate sector employees by Ford et al. (1983).

Significant variation in scores on the second subscale of the M.J.B.I. was apparent in different work locations. Work locations with the highest average scores on this subscale were those sharing common features of task complexity, uncertainty, and high levels of change. The significant differences in subscale scores between occupational groups and work locations, together with the significant predictors of these subscales revealed in a multiple regression analysis tentatively suggest that further investigation of the relationship between burnout and the quality of supervisor/subordinate communication processes in the R.C.A. will reveal a causal link between burnout and dysfunctional organisation communication processes in corporate sector organisations.

Tentative support was found for Frustration, Exhaustion and Defeat being a late stage in the development sequence of burnout. As this is a major component in the model of burnout proposed by Golembiewski et al. (1983) it is suggested that the model could be further refined using a burnout instrument designed to reliably assess burnout in organisational settings.

Multiple regression analysis revealed that perceived adequacy of task related communication, a variable reflecting components of several previously reported significant predictors of burnout among human service workers, was a consistently more powerful predictor of each of the subscales of the M.J.B.I. associated with burnout than any other variable. Results suggest that the experience of burnout in the R.C.A., insofar as it has been measured by the M.J.B.I., reflects the cumulative effects of role ambiguity. Burnout can thus be conceptualized partly as the product of a systemic organisational communication dysfunction to a greater extent than the incapacity of individuals to cope with stress arising from performance of the work itself although this undoubtedly contributes differentially as a function of individual differences in coping.

The correlational nature of the study design did not permit the development of adequate causal hypotheses. Results of the regression analysis suggest however that further exploration of the relationship between burnout and task related communication could yield useful causal insights and assist in the development of an operationalizable model of the burnout process in organisations.

The causes of burnout probably with justification, have been ascribed in the literature to a diverse range of individual and organisational factors. It seems unlikely that a precise causal explanation of the negative feelings associated with burnout will be established capable of explaining more than a modest proportion of total variance in the phenomenon. Allowing for the effects of common method variance in the present study; a predictive correlate accounting for twenty four per cent of total variance in Frustration, Exhaustion and Defeat must be considered to have relevance to further more rigorous research in burnout among corporate sector populations.

Methodological Limitations of the Present Study

The present study was an exploratory investigation of burnout and its relationship to other work variables common in large organisational settings and previously found to be related to burnout among human service workers. The design of the study was determined by the broader context and the practical limitations of the Equal Employment Opportunity Survey within which it occured. Cross sectional data was obtained from a representative sample of employees in a single organisation to shed some light on what is essentially a process occuring over time to facilitate the formulation of more specific research questions concerning the nature and aetiology of burnout in corporate sector organisations. The limitations of using such cross sectional data to model a cyclic set of events is not inconsiderable.

Interpretation of the present results is limited by the problems of single organisation sample representativeness and the survey methodology. Although no specific causal framework has been offered the correlational nature of the study allows for alternative explanations to those offered here. The possibility that common method variance was responsible for the magnitude of correlations is a particularly relevant caveat since all data used in the analysis was derived from the same questionnaire albeit one in which the item format has varied to minimize the effects of response set. Substantially related to the problem of potential method variance is the tendency for respondents to have maintained consistency of response across the E.E.O. survey questionnaire which preceded the M.J.B.I. and the burnout items themselves.

Longitudinal data is required ideally utilizing different methods of assessing the experience of burnout to trace those events relevant to its development before any reliable causal explanation of the phenomenon can be attempted. This raises some problems in the measurement of burnout as more objective behavioural indices are yet to be developed. The identification of reliable behavioural indices of burnout will require further research of a more experimental nature than has so far been the case to determine precisely which variables constitute the concept at different stages of its development.

REFERENCE NOTES

1. American Psychiatric Association. Burnout: a bibliography.
    Prepared for the Hospital and Community Psychiatric Service,
    December, 1982.

2. University of Melbourne Library. Burnout: a literature search.
    March, 1985.

3. Morris, M.J. Equal employment opportunity survey in the RCA :
    Report summarizing data collected from female and male employees
    of the RCA. Unpublished manuscript, June 1986. (Available from
    M. J. Morris, 23 Fairy Street, Ivanhoe, Victoria, 3079).

REFERENCE LIST

Bandura, A. Self efficacy : toward a unifying theory of behavioral change. Psychological Review, 1977, 84, 191-215.

Belcastro, P.A. Gold, R.S. & Hays, L.C. Maslach Burnout Inventory : factor structures for samples of teachers. Psychological Reports, 1983, 53, 364-366.

Berkeley Planning Associates. Evaluation of child abuse and neglect, demonstration project 1974/1977: Vol. 9. Project management and Worker burnout: final report, Springfield, VA: National Technical Information Service, 1977.

Billings, A.G. & Moos, R.H. Work Stress and the stress-buffering roles of work and family resources. Journal of Occupational Behaviour, 1982, 3, 215-232.

Cardinell, C. Burnout? Midlife Crisis? Let's understand ourselves. Contemporary Education, 1981, 52, 103-108.

Draper, N.R. & Smith, H. Applied regression analysis. New York : John Wiley, 1966.

Edelwich, J. & Brodsky, A. Burnout : stages of disillusionment in the helping professions. New York : Human Services Press, 1980.

Einsiedel, A. & Tully, A. Methodological considerations in studying the burnout phenomenon. In J. Jones (Ed.), The burnout syndrome: current research, theory, interventions. Park Ridge,Ill.: London House, 1981.

Etzion, D. Moderating effect of social support on the stress-burnout relationship. Journal of Applied Psychology, 1984, 69 (4), 615-622.

Farber, B.A. (Ed.). Stress and burnout in the human service professions. New York : Pergamon Press, 1983.

Farber, B.A. & Heifetz, L.J. The process and dimension of burnout in psychotherapists. Professional Psychology, 1982, 13, 293-301.

Folkman, S. An approach to the measurement of coping. Journal of Occupational Behaviour, 1982, 13, 95-107.

Ford, D.L., Murphy, C.J. & Edwards, K.L. Exploratory development and validation of a Perceptual Job Burnout Inventory: comparison of corporate sector and human service professionals. Psychological Reports, 1983, 52, 995-1006.

Freudenberger, H.J. Staff burnout. Journal of Social Issues, 1974, 30(1), 159-165.

Galbraith, J. Designing complex organizations. Reading, MA: Addison Wesley, 1973.

Gann, M.L. The role of personality factors and job characteristics in burnout : a study of social service workers. Dissertation Abstracts International, 1979, 34(07B), 3366.

Ganster, D.C., Mayes, B.T., Sime, W.E. & Tharp, G.D. Managing organizational stress : a field experiment. Journal of Applied Psychology, 1982, 67, (S), 533-542.

Golembiewski, R.T. Mid-life transition and mid-career crisis: a special case for individual development. Public Administration Review, 1978, 38, 215-222.

Golembiewski, R.T., Munzenrider, R. & Carter, D. Phases of progressive burnout and their work site covariants: critical issues in OD research and praxis. The Journal of Applied Behavioral Science, 1983, 19, 461-481.

Gowler, D. & Legge, K. (Eds.). Managerial stress. Epping, United Kingdom: Grower Press, 1975.

Hackman, D. & Oldham, G. Development of the Job Diagnostic Survey. Journal of Applied Psychology, 1975, 60, 159-170.

Jackson, S. Participation in decision-making as a strategy for reducing job related strain. Journal of Applied Psychology, 1983, 68, 3-19.

Kahn, R.L. Conflict, ambiguity and overload: three elements in job stress. Occupational Mental Health, 1973, 3, 2-9.

Kearns, J.L. Stress in industry. London: Priory Press, 1973.

Keenan, A. & Newton, T.J. Stressful events stressors and psychological strains in young professional engineers. Journal of Occupational Behaviour, 1985, 6, 151-156.

Kerlinger, F.N. & Pedhazur, E.J. Multiple regression in behavioral research. New York : Holt, Rinehart and Winston Inc., 1973.

Maslach, C. 'Burned out'. Human Behaviour, 1976, 5, 16-22.

Maslach, C., & Jackson, S.E. The measurement of experienced burnout. Journal of Occupational Behaviour, 1981, 2, 99-113.

Meier, S.T. Toward a theory of burnout. Human Relations, 1983, 36, (10), 899-910.

Metz, P. An exploratory study of professional burnout and renewal among educators. Dissertation Abstracts International, 1979, 40 (09B), 4568.

Muchinsky, P.M. Organizational communication: relationships to organizational climate and job satisfaction. Academy of Management Journal, 1977, 20, 592-607.

Newman, J.E. & Beehr, T.A. Personal and organizational strategies for handling job stress: a review of research and opinion. Personnel Psychology, 1979, 32, 1-43.

Osipow, S.H., Doty, R.E. & Spokane, A.R. Occupational stress, strain and coping across the life span. Journal of Vocational Behavior, 1985, 27, 98-108.

Osipow, S.H. & Spokane, A.R. A manual for measures of occupational stress, strain and coping. Columbus, Ohio: Marathon Consulting and Press, 1983.

Perlman, B. & Hartman, E.A. Burnout: summary and future research. Human Relations, 1982, 35(4), 283-305.

Pines, A.M., Aronson, E. & Kafry,D. Burnout: from tedium to personal growth. New York: The Free Press, 1981.

Porter, L.W. & Roberts, K.H. Organizational communication. In M. Dunnette (Ed.). Handbook of industrial and organizational psychology. Chicago: Rand-McNally, 1976.

Rummel, R.J. Applied factor analysis. Evanstow: North Western University Press, 1970.

Sharit, J. & Salvendy, G. Occupational stress: review and reappraisal. Human Factors, 1982, 24(2), 129-162.

Snyder, R.A. & Morris, J.H. Organizational communication and performance. Journal of Applied Psychology, 1984, 69, 401-465.

SPSS Inc. A complete guide to SPSS[x] language and operation. New York: McGraw-Hill, 1983.

Stevens, G.B. & O'Neil, P. Expectation and burnout in the developmental disabilities field. American Journal of Community Psychology, 1983, 11, 615-627.

Van Mannen, J. & Katz, R. Individuals and their careers: some temporal considerations for work satisfaction. Personnel Psychology, 1976, 29, 601-616.

Van Sell, M., Brief, A.P. & Schuler, R.S. Role conflict and role ambiguity: integration of the literature and directions for future research. Human Relations, 1981, 34, 43-72.

Veniga, R.L. & Spradley, J.B. The work/stress connection. How to cope with job burnout. New York: Ballantine Inc., 1981.

Victorian Government Information Service. Workcare report. Melbourne: Victorian Government Printing Office, 1986.

APPENDIX A

The Modified Job Burnout Inventory

APPENDIX

EEO STRUCTURED INTERVIEW PLAN

.../ii

.../iii

WHAT SEX ARE YOU?   MALE   FEMALE

HOW OLD ARE YOU?   15-20 YRS   40-44 YRS
(CIRCLE)   21-24 YRS   45-49 YRS
                    25-29 YRS   50-54 YRS
                    30-34 YRS   55 or more
                    35-39 YRS

WHAT COUNTRY WERE YOU BORN IN?

    AUSTRALIA   OVERSEAS (PLEASE SPECIFY)

    _____

WHICH ETHNIC GROUP WOULD YOU DESCRIBE YOURSELF
AS BELONGING TO? e.g. GREEK, AUSTRALIAN ETC.

    _____

IS ENGLISH THE LANGUAGE YOU USE MOST?

            -AT HOME? YES   NO
            -AT WORK? YES   NO

HOW WOULD YOU DESCRIBE YOUR CURRENT MARITAL
STATUS? (CIRCLE)
        SINGLE   WIDOWED
        SEPARATED   MARRIED
        DIVORCED   OTHER

DO YOU HAVE ANY CHILDREN?   YES   NO
            STEPCHILDREN YES   NO

IF NO TO BOTH, PLEASE GO TO Q11.
IF YES TO EITHER PLEASE CONTINUE -

HOW MANY CHILDREN (INCLUDING STEPCHILDREN) DO
YOU HAVE?
            1 2 3 4 5 6 7+ (CIRCLE)

WHAT IS THE AGE OF YOUR YOUNGEST CHILD ___ YRS
                        OLDEST CHILD ___ YRS

10. IN YOUR FAMILY, WHO IS RESPONSIBLE FOR THE
    CHILD CARE ARRANGEMENTS?

                                        TICK
            MYSELF, I AM A SOLE PARENT [ ]
                        MOSTLY MYSELF   [ ]
                    SHARED WITH OTHERS [ ]
                    MOSTLY ANOTHER DOES [ ]

11. ARE YOU A SALARIED   MEMBER OF THE RCA'S
                   [ ]   PERSONNEL?
    WAGES
    [ ]

12. PLEASE INDICATE WHICH OF THE FOLLOWING RANGES
    YOUR SALARY/WAGE FALLS IN BEFORE TAX -

ANNUAL	WEEKLY	HOURLY	TICK
$14,500 or less	$278 or less	$ 7.94 or less	[ ]
$14,501 - $17,500	$279 - $334	$ 7.95 - 9.57	[ ]
$17,501 - $20,500	$335 - $392	$ 9.58 - 11.22	[ ]
$20,501 - $23,500	$393 - $449	$11.23 - 12.86	[ ]
$23,501 - $26,500	$450 - $507	$12.87 - 14.50	[ ]
$26,501 - $29,500	$508 - $564	$14.51 - 16.14	[ ]
$29,501 - $32,500	$565 - $622	$16.15 - 17.79	[ ]
$32,501 - $35,500	$623 - $682	$17.80 - 18.95	[ ]
$35,501 - $37,500	$683 - $721	$18.96 - 20.03	[ ]
$37,501 - $40,500	$722 - $779	$20.04 - 21.63	[ ]
$40,501 - $45,000	$780 - $862	$21.64 - 22.69	[ ]
$45,001 - $50,000	$863 - $958	$22.70 - 25.21	[ ]
$50,000 or more	$959 or more	$25.22 or more	[ ]

13. HOW MANY YEARS OF RELEVANT WORK EXPERIENCE DID
    YOU HAVE BEFORE JOINING THE RCA? _____ YRS

14. HOW LONG HAVE YOU BEEN EMPLOYED BY THE RCA?

                                    _____ YRS

15. WHAT IS THE HIGHEST EDUCATION LEVEL YOU HAVE
    ATTAINED? (CIRCLE)

    PRIMARY   APPRENTICESHIP   MASTERS
    FORMS 1-3   CERTIFICATE
    FORM 4   DIPLOMA   PH.D.
    FORM 5   DEGREE   OTHER (SPECIFY)
    HSC   POSTGRAD DIPLOMA   _____

. DO YOU SUFFER FROM ANY PERMANENT OR TEMPORARY DISABILITY WHICH FALLS IN THE FOLLOWING CATEGORIES? (PLEASE CIRCLE AS MANY AS ARE APPLICABLE)

AN IMPAIRMENT IN -	SEVERE	MODERATE	MILD
* HEARING	1	2	3
* SIGHT	1	2	3
* MOVEMENT DIFFICULTIES	1	2	3
* DIFFICULTY USING HANDS (INCLUDING RSI)	1	2	3
* PHYSICAL APPEARANCE	1	2	3
* MENTAL/INTELLECTUAL	1	2	3
* OTHER-INCLUDING CHRONIC ILLNESS/PAIN (SPECIFY) _____	1	2	3

. DID YOU SUFFER FROM ANY IMPAIRMENT OF THIS NATURE UPON COMMENCING WORK FOR THE RCA?

YES   NO

. WHAT TYPE OF POSITION DO YOU HOLD IN THE RCA e.g. SECRETARY, ENGINEER etc? _____

. WHICH LOCATION DO YOU WORK AT eg. HEAD OFFICE, BENDIGO etc? _____

. WHICH BRANCH DO YOU BELONG TO?

*OPERATIONS-☐   *CORPORATE ADMINISTRATION-☐

*PLANNING & DESIGN-☐   *PERSONNEL & EMPLOYEE RELATIONS-☐

. WHAT SUB-BRANCH DO YOU BELONG TO EG. WORKS, ADMINISTRATION etc?_____

. HAVE YOU APPLIED FOR A PROMOTION WITHIN THE PAST 5 YEARS? (IF YOU HAVE LESS THAN 5 YEARS SERVICE - HAVE YOU APPLIED FOR A PROMOTION SINCE JOINING THE RCA?)

YES   NO

NUMBER OF PROMOTION APPLICATIONS _____

NUMBER OF INTERVIEWS ACHIEVED _____

NUMBER OF TIMES SUCCESSFUL _____

23. IF YOU ARE CURRENTLY NOT APPLYING FOR PROMOTION OR IF YOU HAVE GIVEN UP APPLYING, IS IT FOR ANY OF THE FOLLOWING REASONS? (YOU MAY CIRCLE MORE THAN ONE.)

	CIRCLE
NOT INTERESTED IN PROMOTION_____	1
DO NOT KNOW HOW TO APPLY_____	2
HAVEN'T BEEN IN THE JOB LONG ENOUGH____	3
HAVE NOT BEEN ENCOURAGED TO APPLY_____	4
LITTLE CHANCE OF GETTING A PROMOTION ___	5
NO OPPORTUNITY FOR PROMOTION IN MY JOB_	6
FAMILY RESPONSIBILITIES ARE TOO DEMANDING	7
HAVE GOT THE SKILLS BUT NO QUALIFICATIONS	8
OTHER (PLEASE SPECIFY)_____ _____	9

24. IF YOU WERE INTERVIEWED IN CONNECTION WITH YOUR PRESENT POSITION, WERE YOU ASKED QUESTIONS ABOUT ANY OF THE FOLLOWING AT THE INTERVIEW, AND DID YOU CONSIDER THE QUESTIONS TO BE INAPPROPRIATE?

	NOT ASKED	ASKED, NOT CONCERNED	ASKED, NOT APPROPRIATE	DON'T REMEMBER
*YOUR AGE	1	2	3	4
*YOUR ETHNIC ORIGIN	1	2	3	4
*YOUR MARITAL STATUS	1	2	3	4
*YOUR PRIVATE LIFE	1	2	3	4
*YOUR SPOUSE/PARTNERS OCCUPATION	1	2	3	4
*YOUR SPOUSE/PARTNERS ATTITUDE TO YOUR WORKING	1	2	3	4
*POSSIBILITY OF FUTURE CHILDREN	1	2	3	4
*NUMBER & AGES OF YOUR CHILDREN	1	2	3	4
*FAMILY RESPONSIBILITY	1	2	3	4
*YOUR POLITICAL VIEWS	1	2	3	4
*YOUR RELIGIOUS VIEWS	1	2	3	4

25. IF YOU HAVE APPLIED FOR A PROMOTION, RATE YOUR EXPERIENCE OF THE FOLLOWING SELECTION PROCEDURES (IF YOU HAVE NEVER APPLIED FOR A PROMOTION, RATE EACH PROCEDURE ACCORDING TO WHAT YOU HAVE HEARD FROM OTHERS).

(CIRCLE)

	VERY SATISFACTORY	ADEQUATE	LESS THAN ADEQUATE
*AVAILABILITY OF UP TO DATE JOB DESCRIPTION	1	2	3
*THE QUALITY & RELEVANCE OF THE INTERVIEW PANEL	1	2	3
*THE INTERVIEW ITSELF	1	2	3
*THE LENGTH OF TIME TAKEN FROM ADVERTISEMENT TO APPOINTMENT	1	2	3
*COMMUNICATION OF OUTCOME TO SUCCESSFUL & UNSUCCESS-FUL APPLICANTS	1	2	3
*THE APPEALS PROCEDURE	1	2	3
*THE OVERALL PROMOTION PROCEDURE	1	2	3

26. DO YOU THINK IT IS MORE DIFFICULT FOR A WOMAN TO BE SUCCESSFULLY PROMOTED IN THE RCA?

(CIRCLE)

*YES, IN ALL CASES   4
*YES, IN MOST CASES   3
*YES, IN SOME CASES   2
*NO, IT IS NOT MORE
 DIFFICULT FOR A
 WOMAN TO BE PROMOTED   1

27. IF YOU CONSIDER THAT IT MAY BE MORE DIFFICULT FOR WOMEN TO OBTAIN PROMOTION IN THE RCA, PLACE A TICK (✓) IN ONE OR MORE OF THE FOLLOWING BOXES -

WOMEN HAVE LESS RELEVANT EXPERIENCE. ☐
WOMEN ARE LESS WELL QUALIFIED.......... ☐
WOMEN ARE LESS CONFIDENT.............. ☐
WOMEN ARE LESS ACCEPTABLE TO MALE
                          COLLEAGUES... ☐
WOMEN ARE VIEWED AS LESS CAREER
                         ORIENTATED..... ☐
WOMEN ARE NOT AS WELL INFORMED
            REGARDING CAREER OPTIONS..... ☐
WOMEN ARE ACTIVELY DISCOURAGED FROM
                    SEEKING PROMOTION.. ☐

WOMEN RECEIVE LESS ENCOURAGEMENT
          FROM MANAGEMENT THAN MEN.. ☐
WOMEN HAVE LESS ACCESS TO RELEVANT
                TRAINING THAN MEN···· ☐
OTHER (PLEASE SPECIFY) _____ ☐

28. IN THE PAST 3 YEARS, HAS YOUR SUPERVISOR ENCOURAGED YOU TO APPLY FOR A PROMOTION?

TICK

MY SUPERVISOR HAS OFTEN ENCOURAGED ME ☐
MY SUPERVISOR HAS OCCASIONALLY
                     ENCOURAGED ME ☐
MY SUPERVISOR HAS NEVER ENCOURAGED ME ☐
MY SUPERVISOR HAS DISCOURAGED ME FROM
            APPLYING FOR PROMOTION ☐
I AM NOT INTERESTED IN APPLYING FOR
                        PROMOTION ☐

29. HOW SATISFIED ARE YOU WITH THE ENCOURAGEMENT YOU HAVE RECEIVED FROM YOUR SUPERVISOR IN THIS REGARD? (CIRCLE)

1   VERY PLEASED
2   MOSTLY SATISFIED
3   MIXED FEELINGS
4   MOSTLY DISSATISFIED
5   VERY UNHAPPY

30. WHICH OF THE FOLLOWING STATEMENTS BEST DESCRIBES YOUR KNOWLEDGE OF THE TRAINING PROGRAMS OFFERED IN THE RCA?

TICK

• I HAVE NO KNOWLEDGE OF RCA TRAINING PROGRAMS ☐
• I WAS AWARE OF THE EXISTENCE OF TRAINING PROGRAMS BUT HAVE NO KNOWLEDGE OF THEIR SCOPE AND CONTENT _____ ☐
• I WAS AWARE OF THE EXISTENCE OF TRAINING PROGRAMS AND HAVE SOME KNOWLEDGE OF THEIR SCOPE AND CONTENT _____ ☐
• I AM REGULARLY INFORMED OF RELEVANT TRAINING PROGRAMS AS THEY BECOME AVAILABLE _____ ☐

31. SINCE JOINING THE RCA MY TRAINING NEEDS HAVE BEEN -

TICK

• REGULARLY REVIEWED WITH MY SUPERVISOR.. ☐
• OCCASIONALLY DISCUSSED WITH SUPERVISOR ☐
• LARGELY IGNORED BY RCA .... ☐

32. HOW MANY RCA TRAINING COURSES HAVE YOU ATTENDED IN THE PAST 3 YEARS_____

   HOW MANY EXTERNAL TRAINING COURSES HAVE YOU ATTENDED IN THE PAST 3 YEARS_____

   WHAT IS YOUR ESTIMATE OF THE TOTAL NUMBER OF DAYS YOU HAVE SPENT IN OFF-THE-JOB TRAINING IN THE PAST 3 YEARS_____ DAYS

33. RATE THE ADEQUACY OF EACH ASPECT OF YOUR TRAINING EXPERIENCE ACCORDING TO THE FOLLOWING SCALE - (CIRCLE)

   5   SATISFIED IN MOST RESPECTS
   4   SATISFIED IN SOME RESPECTS
   3   SATISFIED IN VERY FEW RESPECTS
   2   DISSATISFIED IN SOME RESPECTS
   1   DISSATISFIED IN MOST RESPECTS

*THE INDUCTION TRAINING I RECEIVED WHEN I FIRST JOINED THE RCA_____

*THE 'ON THE JOB' TRAINING I HAVE RECEIVED____

*THE OPPORTUNITY I HAVE HAD TO DEVELOP MY SKILL BY ATTENDANCE AT TRAINING COURSES____

*THE EFFORT MY SUPERVISOR MAKES TO ENSURE I AM ADEQUATELY TRAINED FOR MY JOB____

*MY PROSPECTS OF RECEIVING THE KIND OF TRAINING THAT WILL ASSIST ME TO MAKE PROGRESS IN THE RCA____

*THE QUALITY OF THE TRAINING COURSES I HAVE ATTENDED IN THE RCA (IF ANY)____

*THE AMOUNT AND QUALITY OF INFORMATION I RECEIVE CONCERNING TRAINING AVAILABLE IN THE RCA____

*THE EXTENT TO WHICH I HAVE BEEN CONSULTED BY MY SUPERVISOR CONCERNING MY CAREER ASPIRATIONS AND TRAINING NEEDS____

*THE RELEVANCE TO ME OF THE INTERNAL TRAINING COURSES OFFERED BY THE RCA (WHERE THESE ARE KNOWN)____

*THE EXTENT TO WHICH THE RCA PROVIDES EQUAL OPPORTUNITY OF ACCESS TO/AVAILABLE TRAINING.____

*THE OVERALL QUALITY OF TRAINING AVAILABLE IN THE RCA TO PEOPLE DOING THE TYPE OF WORK I DO____

*THE STUDY LEAVE PROVISIONS IN THE RCA____

*HOW WELL HAS YOUR TRAINING PREPARED YOU FOR PROMOTION IN THE RCA____

34. HOW IMPORTANT DO YOU CONSIDER CAREER DEVELOPMENT FOR YOUR LONG TERM SATISFACTION AT WORK?

   TICK

   PROGRESS IN MY CAREER IS VERY IMPORTANT TO ME

   OF SOME IMPORTANCE BUT NOT MY PRINCIPAL REASON FOR WORKING AT THE RCA____

   CAREER DEVELOPMENT IS OF VERY LITTLE IMPORTANCE TO ME____

35. HOW WELL TRAINED DO YOU FEEL YOU ARE NOW TO UNDERTAKE YOUR CURRENT RESPONSIBILITIES? TICK

   *VERY ADEQUATELY TRAINED IN ALL RESPECTS....
   *ADEQUATELY TRAINED IN MOST RESPECTS......
   *LACKING SKILLS IN ONE AREA OF MY WORK....
   *LACKING SKILLS IN SEVERAL IMPORTANT AREAS OF MY WORK ....

36. HOW IMPORTANT IS ADEQUATE TRAINING LIKELY TO BE IN DETERMINING WHETHER OF NOT YOU OBTAIN A PROMOTION FROM YOUR PRESENT POSITION? (TICK)

   *VERY IMPORTANT.
   *OF SOME IMPORTANCE, BUT PROBABLY NOT CRUCIAL.
   *NOT AT ALL IMPORTANT.

37. HOW SATISFIED ARE YOU WITH YOUR PROSPECTS FOR FUTURE CAREER DEVELOPMENT IN THE RCA? (TICK)

   ●VERY PLEASED   ●MOSTLY SATISFIED....
   ● MIXED FEELINGS   ●MOSTLY DISSATISFIED
   ● VERY UNHAPPY

38. OVERALL, HOW PLEASED ARE YOU WITH YOUR PRESENT JOB? (TICK)

*PLEASED ☐   *MOSTLY SATISFIED ☐
*MIXED FEELINGS ☐   *MOSTLY DISSATISFIED ☐
*VERY UNHAPPY ☐

39. WITH REGARD TO YOUR LEVEL OF RESPONSIBILITY, DO YOU FEEL YOU ARE GIVEN TOO MUCH, TOO LITTLE OR ABOUT THE RIGHT LEVEL OF RESPONSIBILITY? (✓)

*I AM CAPABLE OF TAKING MORE RESPONSIBILITY IN MY PRESENT JOB ☐
*I HAVE ABOUT THE RIGHT AMOUNT OF RESPONSIBILITY IN MY JOB ☐
*I FEEL I AM GIVEN TOO MUCH RESPONSIBILITY ☐

40. HOW EASY IS IT FOR EMPLOYEES TO OBTAIN ADEQUATE CAREER GUIDANCE IN THE RCA?

(TICK)

*ADVICE ON CAREER DEVELOPMENT IS READILY AVAILABLE TO ALL EMPLOYEES IN THE RCA... ☐
*CAREER GUIDANCE IS EASILY AVAILABLE FOR SOME AND DIFFICULT FOR OTHERS TO OBTAIN. ☐
*CAREER GUIDANCE IS DIFFICULT FOR MOST EMPLOYEES TO OBTAIN UNLESS THEY ARE PARTICULARLY AMBITIOUS AND PERSISTENT.... ☐
*IT IS DIFFICULT IF NOT IMPOSSIBLE FOR EMPLOYEES TO OBTAIN HELPFUL CAREER GUIDANCE IN THE RCA................. ☐

41. HOW SATISFIED ARE YOU WITH THE WAYS IN WHICH YOU HAVE BEEN COUNSELLED AND ASSISTED IN DEVELOPING YOUR CAREER IN THE RCA? (PLEASE ANSWER THIS QUESTION IN RELATION TO THE ASSISTANCE YOU HAVE RECEIVED IN THE LAST 3 YEARS) (TICK)

*VERY PLEASED ☐   *MOSTLY SATISFIED ☐
*MIXED FEELINGS ☐   *MOSTLY DISSATISFIED ☐
*VERY UNHAPPY ☐

42. BELOW IS A LIST OF REASONS OFTEN GIVEN BY PEOPLE TO EXPLAIN WHY THEY JOINED THE WORKFORCE. COULD YOU PLEASE RANK EACH ONE ACCORDING TO HOW IMPORTANT IT IS FOR YOUR OWN DECISION TO JOIN AND REMAIN IN THE WORKFORCE. E.G. 1 = MOST IMPORTANT REASON FOR ME - 8 = LEAST IMPORTANT REASON FOR ME. (PLACE ONLY ONE NUMBER IN EACH BOX, PLEASE RANK EACH SUGGESTION AND DO NOT USE THE SAME NUMBER TWICE)

*TO SUPPORT MYSELF ☐
*TO SUPPORT MY FAMILY ☐
*TO PROVIDE A SECOND FAMILY INCOME ☐
*TO HAVE A STABLE CAREER ☐
*TO HAVE INTERESTING WORK ☐
*TO HAVE AN OUTLET OUTSIDE THE HOME ENVIRONMENT ☐
*TO PROVIDE EXTRA OR LUXURY ITEMS FOR MYSELF & MY FAMILY ☐
*OTHER (PLEASE SPECIFY)_____ ☐

43. WOULD YOU CHOOSE TO TAKE A PERMANENT PART TIME JOB IF IT WERE AVAILABLE? (TICK)

*YES, FOR A FEW YEARS, PROVIDED I CAN RETURN TO FULL TIME WORK ☐
*YES, IF PROMOTION OPPORTUNITIES AND OTHER BENEFITS WERE RETAINED ☐
*YES, EVEN IF PROMOTION OPPORTUNITIES AND OTHER BENEFITS WERE NOT RETAINED ☐
*NO, I COULDN'T LIVE ON A LOWER INCOME ☐
*NO, I AM NOT INTERESTED IN PART TIME WORK ☐
*NO, NOT AT PRESENT, BUT I MIGHT LATER ON ☐
*OTHER, PLEASE COMMENT_____ ☐

*IF YES, HOW MANY HOURS PER WEEK WOULD YOU LIKE TO WORK? _____ HRS/WK.

44. HAVE YOU EVER BEEN GIVEN ADDITIONAL DUTIES NORMALLY HANDLED BY A MORE SENIOR OFFICER WHEN THAT PERSON IS ABSENT?   YES   NO

45. DID YOU RECEIVE A HIGHER DUTIES ALLOWANCE FOR THESE ADDITIONAL DUTIES? (✓)

NEVER   SOMETIMES   ALWAYS   NOT APPLICABLE
☐   ☐   ☐   ☐

16. BELOW IS A LIST OF ITEMS RELATING TO ASPECTS
OF YOUR WORKING ENVIRONMENT IN THE RCA. COULD
YOU PLEASE RATE EACH ONE OF THEM ON THE
FOLLOWING SCALE ACCORDING TO HOW YOU FEEL
ABOUT THAT ASPECT OF WORK. (PLEASE PLACE THE
APPROPRIATE SCALE NUMBER IN THE BOX NEXT TO
THAT ITEM)

       1 = TERRIBLE
       2 = VERY UNHAPPY
       3 = UNHAPPY
       4 = MOSTLY DISSATISFIED
       5 = MIXED FEELINGS (EQUALLY SATISFIED
                 & DISSATISFIED)
       6 = MOSTLY SATISFIED
       7 = PLEASED
       8 = VERY PLEASED
       9 = DELIGHTED

 *THE PHYSICAL CONDITIONS IN WHICH YOU WORK
   e.g. SPACE, NOISE LEVEL, TEMPERATURE, SAFETY
   PRECAUTIONS ETC. ☐

 * MATERNITY LEAVE ☐

 * PATERNITY LEAVE ☐

 * THE AMOUNT OF INFORMATION PROVIDED ABOUT THE
   SUPERANNUATION SCHEME BEFORE YOU DECIDED
   WHETHER OR NOT TO JOIN ☐

 * THE DEGREE TO WHICH YOU FULLY UNDERSTAND THE
   PROVISIONS OF YOUR SUPERANNUATION SCHEME (IF
   YOU JOINED) e.g. GENERAL PROVISIONS, LEAVE
   CONDITIONS, DEATH & DISABILITY PROVISIONS
   WITHDRAWAL FROM SERVICE CONDITIONS & LIMITED
   BENEFITS ETC ☐

 * YOUR CURRENT LEVEL OF PAY/SALARY ☐

 * THE HOURS YOU WORK ☐

 * THE AMOUNT OF FLEXIBILITY YOU HAVE REGARDING
   THE HOURS IN WHICH YOU WORK ☐

 * THE TYPE OF WORK YOU DO ☐

 * THE EXTENT TO WHICH YOU FIND YOUR WORK
   INTERESTING AND ABSORBING ☐

 * THE AMOUNT OF WORK EXPECTED FROM YOU BY YOUR
   PRESENT SUPERVISOR ☐

 * THE EFFECTIVENESS OF COMMUNICATION ABOUT WORK
   RELATED ISSUES BETWEEN STAFF & MANAGEMENT IN
   YOUR AREA OF WORK ☐

 * THE EFFECTIVENESS OF COMMUNCIATION BETWEEN
   CO-WORKERS ABOUT WORK RELATED ISSUES IN YOUR
   AREA ☐

 * YOUR ABILITY TO SET YOUR OWN TASK PRIORITIES
   IN YOUR PRESENT JOB ☐

 * YOUR WORKING RELATIONSHIP WITH YOUR
   SUPERVISOR ☐

 * THE QUALITY OF SUPERVISION PROVIDED BY YOUR
   SUPERVISOR ☐

 * THE ABILITY OF YOUR SUPERVISOR TO MAKE FAIR &
   REASONABLE RECOMMENDATIONS ABOUT YOUR PROMOT-
   ABILITY BASED ON YOUR WORK PERFORMANCE ☐

47. TO WHAT EXTENT DO YOU THINK YOUR SUPERVISOR
USES OBJECTIVE CRITERIA (THE QUALITY, SPEED
AND RESOURCE UTILISATION ASPECTS, QUANTITY
OF YOUR WORK) AS OPPOSED TO SUBJECTIVE
CRITERIA (BASED ON YOUR PERSONALITY, YOUR
WORKING RELATIONSHIP WITH HIM/HER, YOUR
REPUTATION & OVERALL CONTRIBUTION) TO MAKE
HIS/HER ASSESSMENTS ABOUT YOUR WORK
PERFORMANCE? (CIRCLE ON NUMBER ON THIS 7 POINT
SCALE)

TOTALLY		EQUAL			TOTALLY	
OBJECTIVE		MIXTURE			SUBJECTIVE	
1	2	3	4	5	6	7

48. HOW WOULD YOU DESCRIBE THE CLARITY OF YOUR
WORK GOALS AND OBJECTIVES AS THEY ARE
COMMUNICATED TO YOU BY YOUR SUPERVISOR OR
THOSE REQUIRING THE WORK? (CIRCLE ONE NUMBER
ON THIS 5 POINT SCALE)

		SOMETIMES		
		CLEAR AND		
ALWAYS	MOSTLY	OTHER TIMES	MOSTLY	ALWAYS
VERY UNCLEAR	UNCLEAR	UNCLEAR	CLEAR	VERY CLEAR
1	2	3	4	5

49. HOW MUCH ATTENTION DOES YOUR SUPERVISOR PAY TO YOUR CURRENT "WORK SITUATION" (EG. THE TYPE AND DETAILS OF JOBS YOU ARE WORKING, ON YOUR CURRENT WORKLOAD AND HOW FAR YOU HAVE PROGRESSED TOWARDS COMPLETION)

MY SUPERVISOR IS: (CIRCLE ONE OF THE FOLLOWING)

1 ALWAYS FULLY AWARE OF MY CURRENT WORK SITUATION
2 USUALLY AWARE OF MY WORK SITUATION
3 AWARE OF SOME ASPECTS, NOT OTHERS
4 PAYS LITTLE ATTENTION TO MY WORK SITUATION
5 PAYS NO ATTENTION TO MY CURRENT WORK SITUATION

50. TO WHAT EXTENT DOES YOUR SUPERVISOR MAKE AN EFFORT TO GIVE YOU FEEDBACK (ENCOURAGEMENT, PRAISE, CONSTRUCTIVE CRITICISM & RECOGNITION) ABOUT YOUR WORK? (CIRCLE A POINT ON THE FOLLOWING SCALE)

HE/SHE NEVER GIVES ME ANY FEEDBACK	SOMETIMES GIVES CONSTRUCTIVE FEEDBACK	HE/SHE GIVES ME ALL THE FEEDBACK I NEED

0	1	2	3	4	5	6	7	8	9

51. HOW DO YOU FEEL ABOUT THE FEEDBACK AND RECOGNITION YOU RECEIVE REGARDING THE EFFORT PUT INTO YOUR WORK AT THE RCA? (CIRCLE)

1 = TERRIBLE
2 = VERY UNHAPPY
3 = UNHAPPY
4 = MOSTLY DISSATISFIED
5 = MIXED FEELINGS (EQUALLY SATISFIED & DISSATISFIED)
6 = MOSTLY SATISFIED
7 = PLEASED
8 = VERY PLEASED
9 = DELIGHTED

52. WHEN THE RCA MAKES A DECISION REGARDING WHICH APPLICANT WILL BE SELECTED FOR A JOB, TO WHAT EXTENT DO YOU THINK THE DECISION RESTS UPON QUALIFICATIONS OR EXPERIENCE? (CIRCLE ONE NUMBER ON THE FOLLOWING SCALE)

MOSTLY QUALS LITTLE ATTENTION TO EXPERIENCE	EQUAL WEIGHTING	MOSTLY EXPERIENCE LITTLE ATTENTION TO QUALS
1	2	3	4	5

53. TO WHAT EXTENT DOES THE NATURE OF YOUR JOB RESULT IN YOU FEELING CUT OFF FROM OTHERS IN THE ORGANISATION? (CIRCLE ONE POINT ON FOLLOWING SCALE)

NEVER	HARDLY EVER	SOMETIMES	FREQUENTLY	ALWAYS
1	2	3	4	5

FEMALES ONLY (Q54 ONLY)

54. DO YOU WORK IN AN AREA WHERE THERE ARE 2 OR LESS FEMALE EMPLOYEES, INCLUDING YOU, REPORTING TO YOUR SUPERVISOR?

YES   NO

IF YES
DO YOU CONSIDER THIS PUTS YOU IN AN ADVANTAGED OR DISADVANTAGED POSITION AS COMPARED TO THE MEN?

*VERY DISADVANTAGED   1
*   DISADVANTAGED   2
*NO DIFFERENCE   (CIRCLE)
  BETWEEN MEN & WOMEN 3
*   ADVANTAGED   4
*   VERY ADVANTAGED   5

PLEASE GIVE BRIEF DETAILS _____

_____
_____

55. IF YOU HAD A PROBLEM OR COMPLAINT REGARDING YOUR WORK AND/OR THE WORK ENVIRONMENT, HOW WOULD YOU FEEL ABOUT APPROACHING THE FOLLOWING PEOPLE FOR ASSISTANCE (PLEASE PLACE A TICK (✓) IN THE APPROPRIATE COLUMN)?

	VERY NEGATIVE	NEGATIVE	NEUTRAL	POSITIVE	VERY POSITIVE
COWORKERS					
SUPERVISOR					
SECTION HEAD					
MIDDLE MANAGEMENT					
SENIOR MANAGEMENT					
PERSONNEL					
TRAINING					
STAFF ASSOCIATION/ UNION					

56. WHAT KIND OF RESPONSE WOULD YOU EXPECT TO GET FROM EACH OF THEM? (USE THE SAME RESPONSE FORMAT AS THAT FOR THE PREVIOUS QUESTIONS).

	VERY NEGATIVE	NEGATIVE	NEUTRAL	POSITIVE	VERY POSITIVE
COWORKERS					
SUPERVISOR					
SECTION HEAD					
MIDDLE MANAGEMENT					
SENIOR MANAGEMENT					
PERSONNEL					
TRAINING					
STAFF ASSOCIATION/ UNION					

IN GENERAL, HOW SATISFIED ARE YOU THAT GRIEVANCES AND PROBLEMS ARE DEALT WITH FAIRLY AND CONSISTENTLY IN THE RCA? (PLEASE CIRCLE)

VERY PLEASED	MOSTLY SATISFIED	MIXED FEELINGS	MOSTLY DISSATISFIED	VERY UNHAPPY
1	2	3	4	5

57. DO YOU THINK THERE ARE ANY "DANGERS" INVOLVED WITH PURSUING A GRIEVANCE IN THE RCA? EG BEING LABELLED AS A TROUBLEMAKER, BEING DISCRIMIN-ATED AGAINST FOR PROMOTION ETC.

TICK

*VERY DEFINITELY THERE ARE DANGERS IN MANY CASES

*IN SOME CASES THERE ARE DANGERS_____

*IN A FEW CASES THERE ARE DANGERS_____

*THERE ARE NO DANGERS IN PURSUING A LEGITIMATE GRIEVANCE IN THE RCA

PLEASE SPECIFY _____

_____

58. IF YOU HAD A GRIEVANCE RELATING TO SEXUAL HARASSMENT DO YOU CONSIDER THE DANGERS OF PURSUING THAT GRIEVANCE COMPARED TO OTHER GRIEVANCES WOULD BE - (CIRCLE)

1 SIGNIFICANTLY INCREASED

2 SOMEWHAT INCREASED

3 ABOUT THE SAME

4 LESS DANGEROUS

5 PURSUING A GRIEVANCE RELATING TO SEXUAL HARASSMENT IS UNLIKELY TO INVOLVE ANY DANGER TO THE COMPLAINANT.

59. HAVE YOU PERSONALLY EXPERIENCED ANY DISCRIMINATION OF DISADVANTAGE IN THE RCA, BECAUSE OF YOUR SEX, REGARDING ANY OF THE FOLLOWING.

*INTERVIEWS FOR NEW POSITIONS__YES/NO

*ALLOCATION OF DUTIES__YES/NO

*STUDY LEAVE___YES/NO

*PARTICIPATION IN DECISION MAKING IN YOUR WORKAREA_____YES/NO

*RANGE OF POSITIONS AVAILABLE_____YES/NO

*DIVISION OF WORKLOAD___YES/NO

*OTHER CONDITIONS OF SERVICE (SPECIFY) _____YES/NO

60. <u>FEMALES ONLY</u>   (Q60 ONLY)

HAVE YOU EXPERIENCED ANY HARSH CRITICISM IN
THE RCA, BASED ON THE FACT THAT YOU WERE -

   *A WORKING WOMAN   YES/NO
   *A WORKING MOTHER   YES/NO/NOT APPLICABLE

61. DO YOU PERSONALLY FEEL THAT YOU HAVE BEEN
    TREATED UNFAIRLY IN THE RCA, IN THE PAST 3
    YEARS, ON ANY OF THE FOLLOWING GROUNDS -
                                    (TICK)

	NEVER	OCCASIONALLY (ONCE/TWICE)	FREQUENTLY	NOT APPLICABLE
YOUR SEX				
YOUR RACE, COLOR, ETHNIC ORIGIN, ACCENT				
YOUR MARITAL STATUS				
PREGNANCY				
PARENTHOOD				
SEXUAL PREFERENCE (HOMOSEXUALITY)				
A PHYSICAL IMPAIRMENT WHICH WOULD NOT AFFECT YOUR JOB PERFORMANCE				
YOUR POLITICAL BELIEFS & ACTIVITIES				
YOUR RELIGIOUS BELIEFS & ACTIVITIES				

62. SEXUAL HARASSMENT COVERS A RANGE OF UNWELCOME,
    UNSOLICITED & NON RECIPROCATED BEHAVIOUR
    WHICH CONSTITUTES DELIBERATE OR UNINTENTIONAL,
    VERBAL OR PHYSICAL CONDUCT OF A SEXUAL NATURE.
    IT EXTENDS FROM UNWELCOME ACTIONS SUCH AS
    GESTURES AND THE DISPLAY OF OFFENSIVE
    PICTURES, COMMENTS OF A SEXUAL NATURE
    IMPLICIT OR EXPLICIT DEMANDS FOR SEXUAL
    ACTIVITIES, TO PHYSICAL CONTACT SUCH AS
    PATTING OR PINCHING THROUGH TO ACTUAL
    MOLESTATION. HARASSMENT MAY OCCUR BY AN
    INDIVIDUAL OR BY A GROUP OF HARASSERS.

    IN THE PAST 3 YEARS HAVE YOU EXPERIENCED
    ANY OF THE FOLLOWING? (CIRCLE 1 OR 2)

	<u>YES</u>	<u>NO</u>
*PEOPLE WORKING IN THE RCA DISPLAYING MAGAZINES OR PICTURES OF A SEXUAL NATURE <u>WHICH YOU FOUND OFFENSIVE</u>	1	2
*PEOPLE WORKING IN THE RCA MAKING <u>REPEATED & UNWELCOME</u> JOKES OR COMMENTS OF A SEXUAL NATURE	1	2
*PEOPLE WORKING IN THE RCA MAKING <u>REPEATED & UNWELCOME</u> PROPOSITIONS, INVITATIONS OR SUGGESTIONS TO YOU OF A SEXUAL NATURE	1	2
*PEOPLE WORKING IN THE RCA MAKING UNWELCOME PHYSICAL CONTACT WITH YOU	1	2
*PEOPLE WORKING IN THE RCA MAKING SEXUAL ADVANCES WITH THE SUGGESTION THAT IF YOU ACCEPT YOUR OPPORTUNITY AT WORK WILL IMPROVE	1	2

    IF YOU HAVE EXPERIENCED SOME FORM
    OF SEXUAL HARASSMENT, DID YOU REPORT
    IT TO, OR DISCUSS IT WITH A PERSON
    IN AUTHORITY?

                          YES = 1
                          NO = 2

<u>IF YES</u>, WERE YOU SATISFIED WITH
THE ACTION TAKEN?

                          YES = 1
                          NO = 2

IF NO, WHY DID YOU NOT REPORT IT?   TICK   COMMENTS (OPTIONAL)_____

*I WAS NOT SUFFICIENTLY UPSET........

*I DEALT WITH IT SUCCESSFULLY MYSELF,   _____

*I DIDN'T KNOW I COULD REPORT IT......

*I WAS AFRAID TO REPORT IT..........   _____

*I THOUGHT REPORTING IT MAY AFFECT

MY JOB PROSPECTS...............   _____

*I THOUGHT NOTHING WOULD BE DONE

ABOUT IT..................   _____

*OTHER (PLEASE SPECIFY)_____

63. THE CURRENT FEDERAL GOVERNMENT POLICIES ON
     EEO ARE TO INCREASE THE REPRESENTATION OF
     WOMEN AND MINORITY GROUPS IN THE WORKFORCE.
     AT PRESENT THERE ARE 2 MAIN TYPES OF STRATEGY
     UTILISED BY DIFFERENT STATES IN ORDER TO
     ACHIEVE THIS, IN ADDITION TO MEASURES WHICH
     DECREASE DISCRIMINATION.

     A. POSITIVE DISCRIMINATION (N.S.W.)
     THIS IS ACHIEVED BY PLACING QUOTAS ON THE
     REPRESENTATION OF A PARTICULAR GROUP IN THE
     WORKFORCE BY A CERTAIN DATE (EG. 50%
     WOMEN BY 1990). SELECTION PROCEDURES UNDER
     THIS SYSTEM THUS TEND TO FAVOUR FEMALE
     APPLICANTS.

     B. AFFIRMATIVE ACTION (VICTORIA)
     WOMEN ARE ACTIVELY ENCOURAGED TO SEEK
     PROMOTION AND QUOTAS ARE PLACED ON TRAINING
     AND EDUCATION COURSES (EG AIM FOR 50%
     WOMEN PER COURSE) IN ORDER TO INCREASE THE
     PROMOTABILITY OR SKILLS OF WOMEN, THUS
     SELECTION PROCEDURES ARE STILL BASED ON
     MERIT.

                                          (TICK)
     WHICH SYSTEM DO YOU FAVOUR?

              A. POSITIVE DISCRIMINATION.

              B. AFFIRMATIVE ACTION.

                        NEITHER.

The following statements relate to some of the ways in which people
experience stress at work. Consider the way in which each statement
applies to the way you feel at work. Place a number between 1 and
6 in the box to the right of each statement according to the following
scale.

1 = Never True
2 = Very Rarely True
3 = Sometimes True
4 = Often True
5 = Very Frequently True
6 = Always True

1.   I cope well with the pressure of my work

2.   No matter what I do, things at work don't seem to
     get better

3.   I cope well with uncertainty at work

4.   I feel used up at the end of the work day

5.   I feel confident about the quality of my work

6.   I feel I give more than I get in return

7.   I feel a sense of isolation from the rest of my peers,
     co-workers etc.

8.   I generally have sufficient time or resources to do my
     job

9.   I feel frustrated by my job

10. I experience conflicting demands in my job

11. I feel uncomfortable stress at work

12. I have difficulty attending to family or personal needs

13. I feel unable to express and share dissatisfaction
     about my job

14. My work load is impossible to catch up

15. My job is such that I can effect little change in the
     work situation

16. Temporarily removing myself from the job environment seems
     to resolve my feelings

ARE THERE ANY ADDITIONAL COMMENTS YOU WOULD LIKE
TO MAKE REGARDING EEO IN THE RCA?

www.ingramcontent.com/pod-product-compliance
Lightning Source LLC
Chambersburg PA
CBHW080845270326
41930CB00013B/3005